FROM NOW ON

MALACHI WARD

Alternative Comics

Stargazer was originally published in *Study Group Magazine 3D*, Henix in *Elfworld #3*, Divination in *Sundays #5*, Negative Space in *Milk and Carrots #2*, Excerpt and Hero of Science in *Mome 22,* The Oviraptor in *Study Group Magazine #1*, Beasts of Kay-7 in *Top Shelf 2.0*, Sweet Dreams in *Smoke Signal #5*, and The Scout in *Hive #3*

Thanks to Erik Aucoin, Marc Arsenault, Dave Pifer, David Ritchie, Julie Pearson, Sean Ford, Jeff Lemire, Farel Dalrymple, Rob Clough, Charles Forsman, Gabe Fowler, Brian Herrick, Alex Kim, Joe Lambert, Eric Reynolds, Jordan Shiveley, Zack Soto, François Vigneault, Leigh Walton, Mom, Dad, Sam, Paul, and of course, Keiko, for being a role model in ways she doesn't know.

Published by **Alternative Comics**
21607B Stevens Creek Blvd.
Cupertino, California 95014
IndyWorld.com

Marc Arsenault, General Manager
David Nuss, Associate Publisher
Erik Aucoin, Commissioning Editor
Laura Susong, Assistant Editor

Printed in the United States of America

ISBN: 978-1-934460-91-7

MalachiWard.com | malachi.ward@gmail.com

TABLE OF CONTENTS

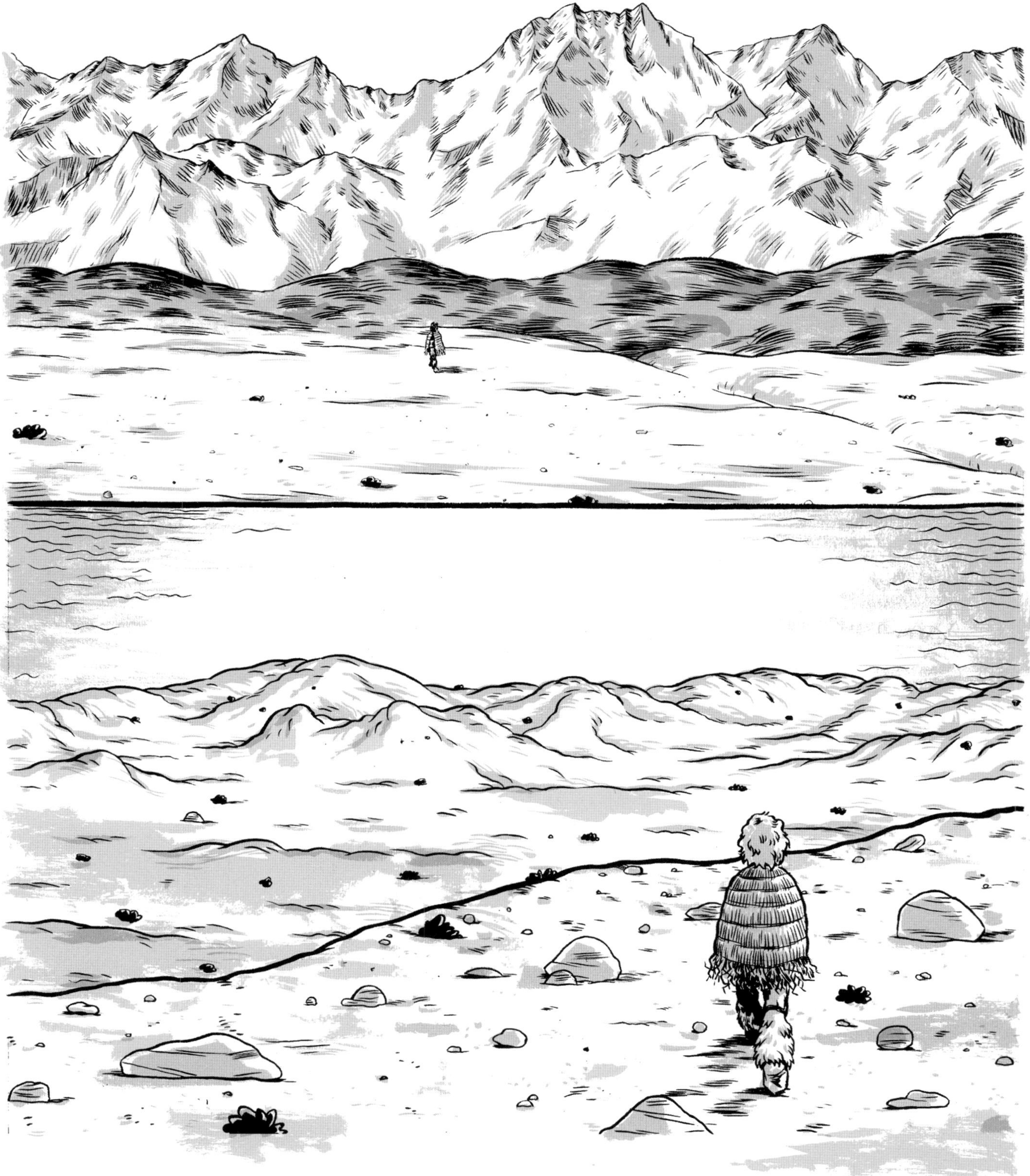

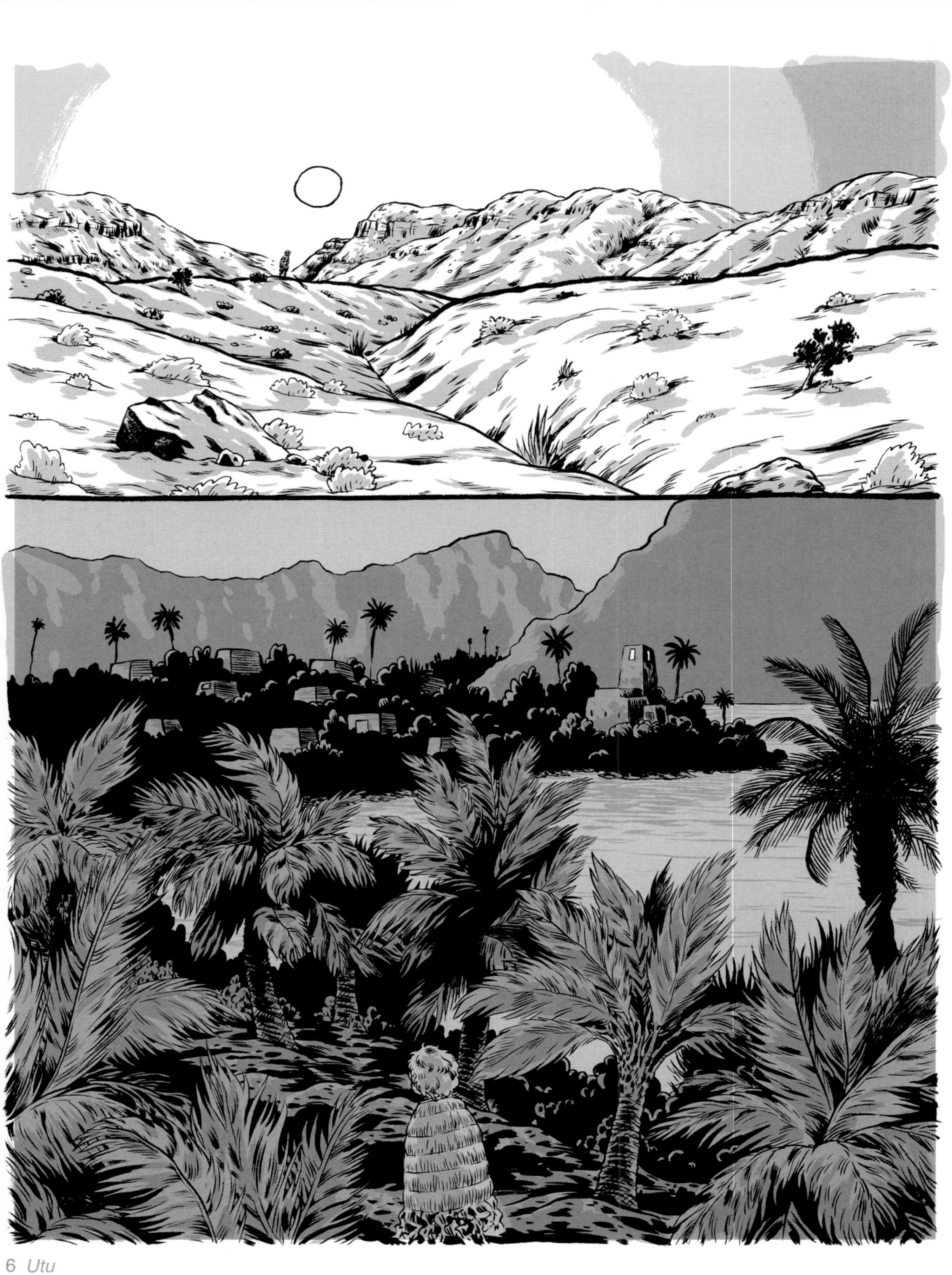

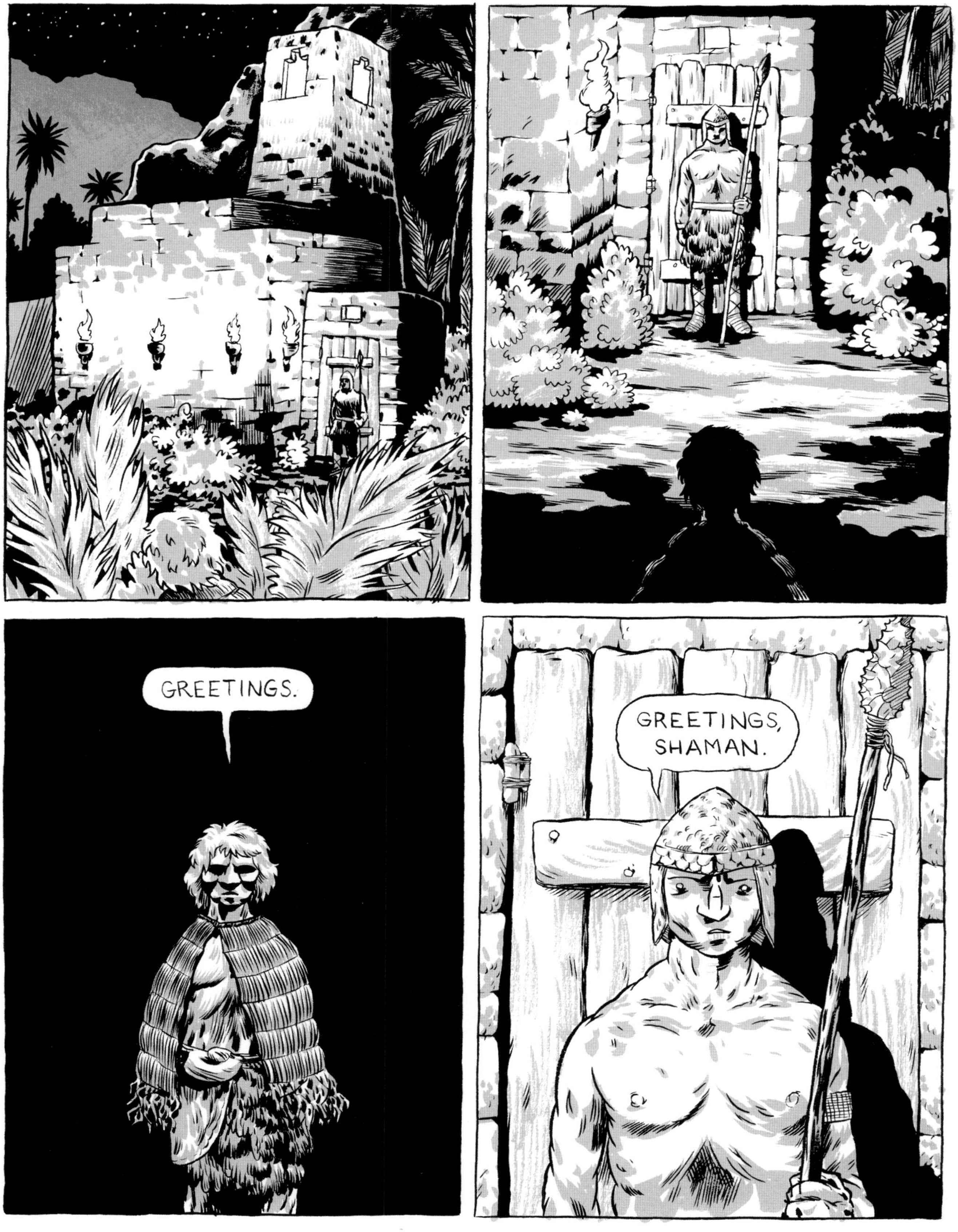
GREETINGS.
GREETINGS, SHAMAN.

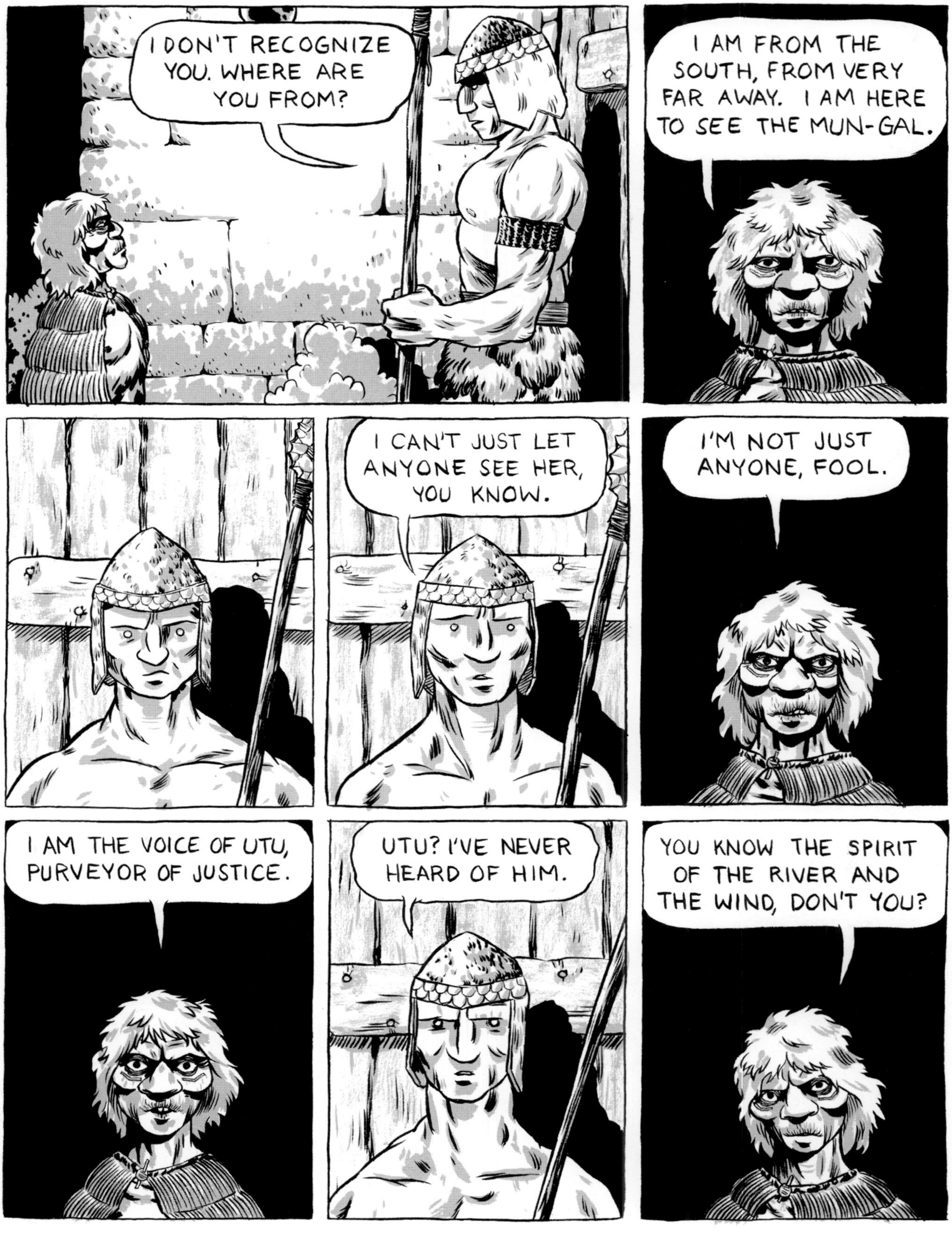
I DON'T RECOGNIZE YOU. WHERE ARE YOU FROM?
I AM FROM THE SOUTH, FROM VERY FAR AWAY. I AM HERE TO SEE THE MUN-GAL.
I CAN'T JUST LET ANYONE SEE HER, YOU KNOW.
I'M NOT JUST ANYONE, FOOL.
I AM THE VOICE OF UTU, PURVEYOR OF JUSTICE.
UTU? I'VE NEVER HEARD OF HIM.
YOU KNOW THE SPIRIT OF THE RIVER AND THE WIND, DON'T YOU?

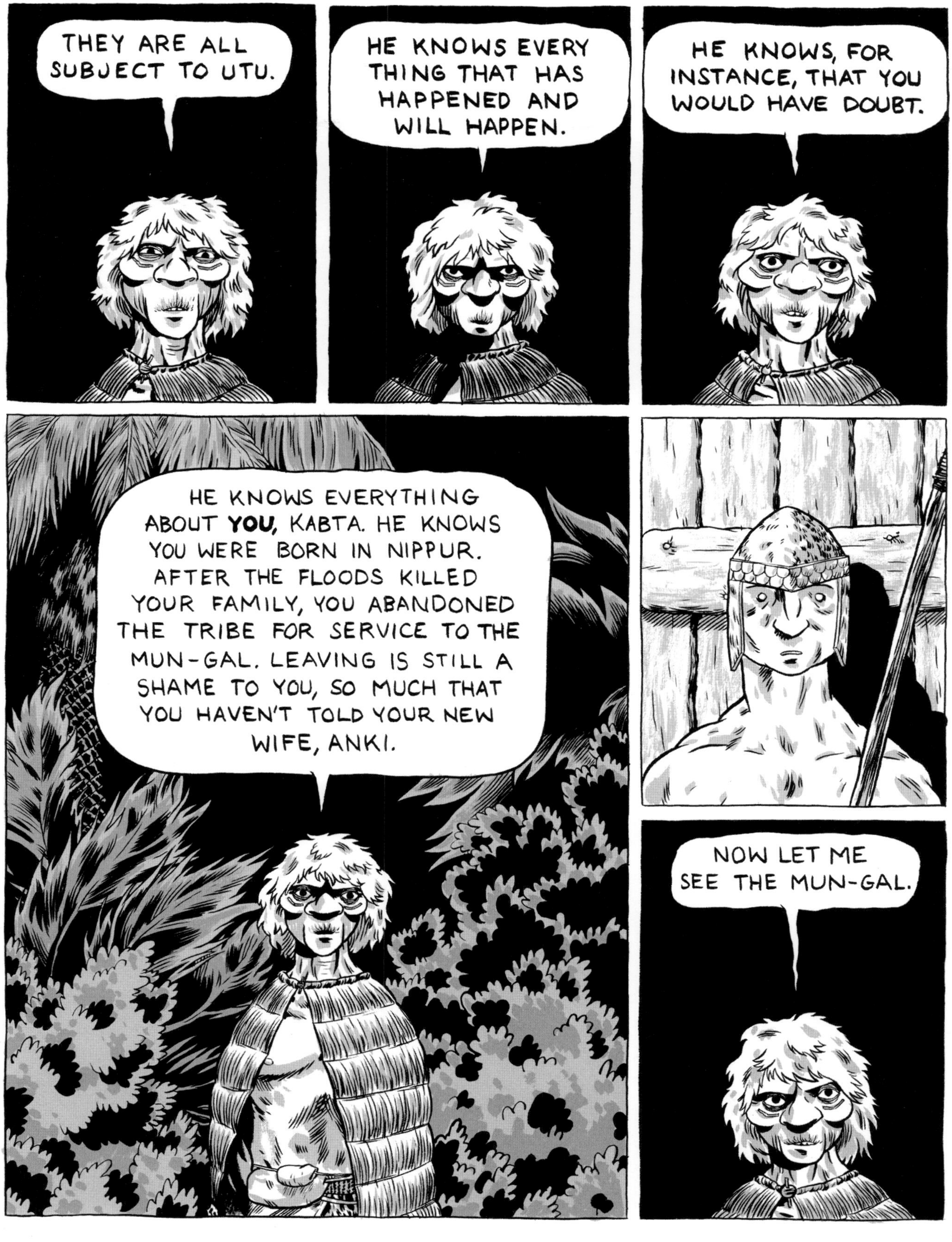
THEY ARE ALL SUBJECT TO UTU.
HE KNOWS EVERY THING THAT HAS HAPPENED AND WILL HAPPEN.
HE KNOWS, FOR INSTANCE, THAT YOU WOULD HAVE DOUBT.
HE KNOWS EVERYTHING ABOUT **YOU,** KABTA. HE KNOWS YOU WERE BORN IN NIPPUR. AFTER THE FLOODS KILLED YOUR FAMILY, YOU ABANDONED THE TRIBE FOR SERVICE TO THE MUN-GAL. LEAVING IS STILL A SHAME TO YOU, SO MUCH THAT YOU HAVEN'T TOLD YOUR NEW WIFE, ANKI.
NOW LET ME SEE THE MUN-GAL.

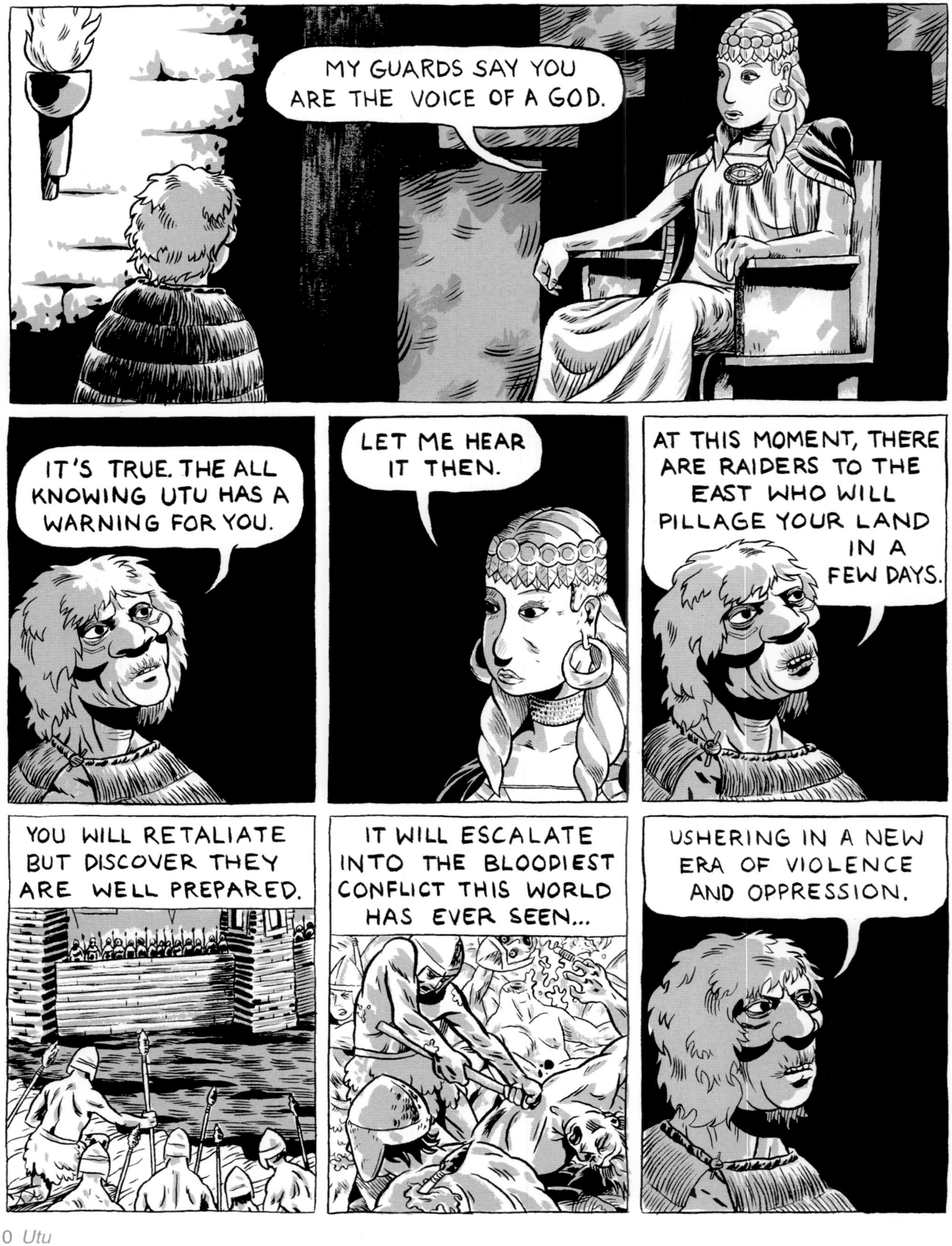
MY GUARDS SAY YOU ARE THE VOICE OF A GOD.
IT'S TRUE. THE ALL KNOWING UTU HAS A WARNING FOR YOU.
LET ME HEAR IT THEN.
AT THIS MOMENT, THERE ARE RAIDERS TO THE EAST WHO WILL PILLAGE YOUR LAND IN A FEW DAYS.
YOU WILL RETALIATE BUT DISCOVER THEY ARE WELL PREPARED.
IT WILL ESCALATE INTO THE BLOODIEST CONFLICT THIS WORLD HAS EVER SEEN...
USHERING IN A NEW ERA OF VIOLENCE AND OPPRESSION.

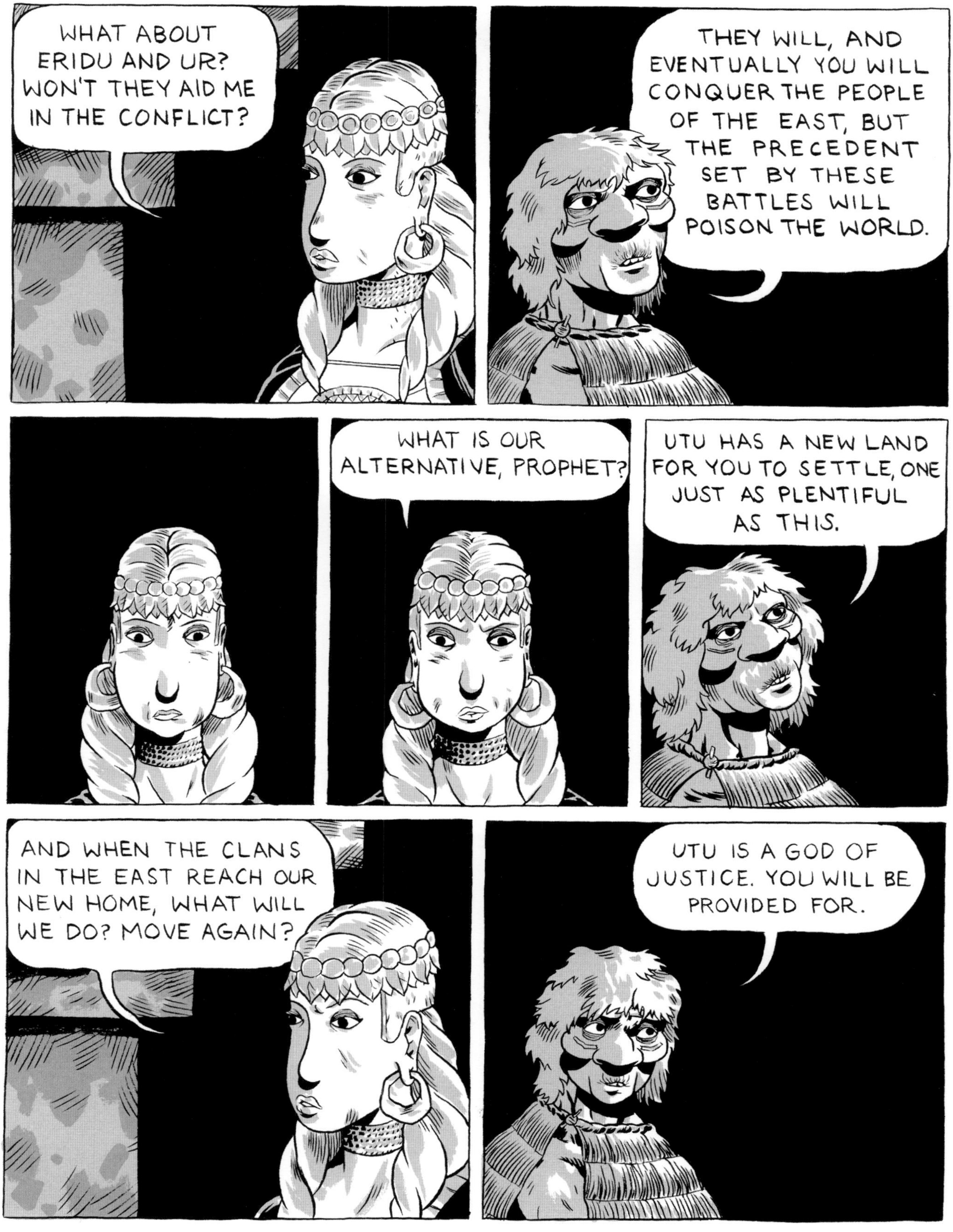
WHAT ABOUT ERIDU AND UR? WON'T THEY AID ME IN THE CONFLICT?
THEY WILL, AND EVENTUALLY YOU WILL CONQUER THE PEOPLE OF THE EAST, BUT THE PRECEDENT SET BY THESE BATTLES WILL POISON THE WORLD.
WHAT IS OUR ALTERNATIVE, PROPHET?
UTU HAS A NEW LAND FOR YOU TO SETTLE, ONE JUST AS PLENTIFUL AS THIS.
AND WHEN THE CLANS IN THE EAST REACH OUR NEW HOME, WHAT WILL WE DO? MOVE AGAIN?
UTU IS A GOD OF JUSTICE. YOU WILL BE PROVIDED FOR.

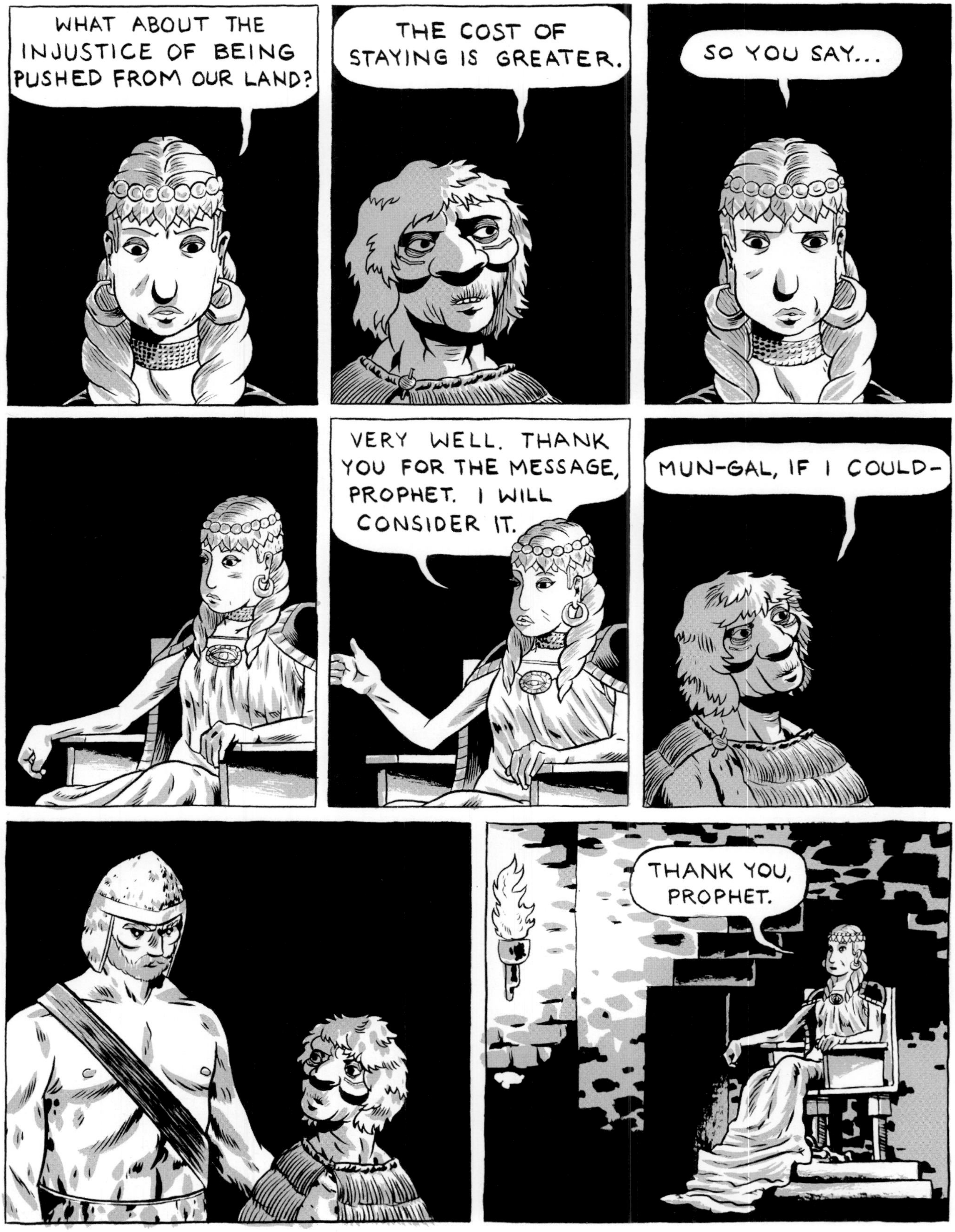
WHAT ABOUT THE INJUSTICE OF BEING PUSHED FROM OUR LAND?
THE COST OF STAYING IS GREATER.
SO YOU SAY...
VERY WELL. THANK YOU FOR THE MESSAGE, PROPHET. I WILL CONSIDER IT.
MUN-GAL, IF I COULD-
THANK YOU, PROPHET.

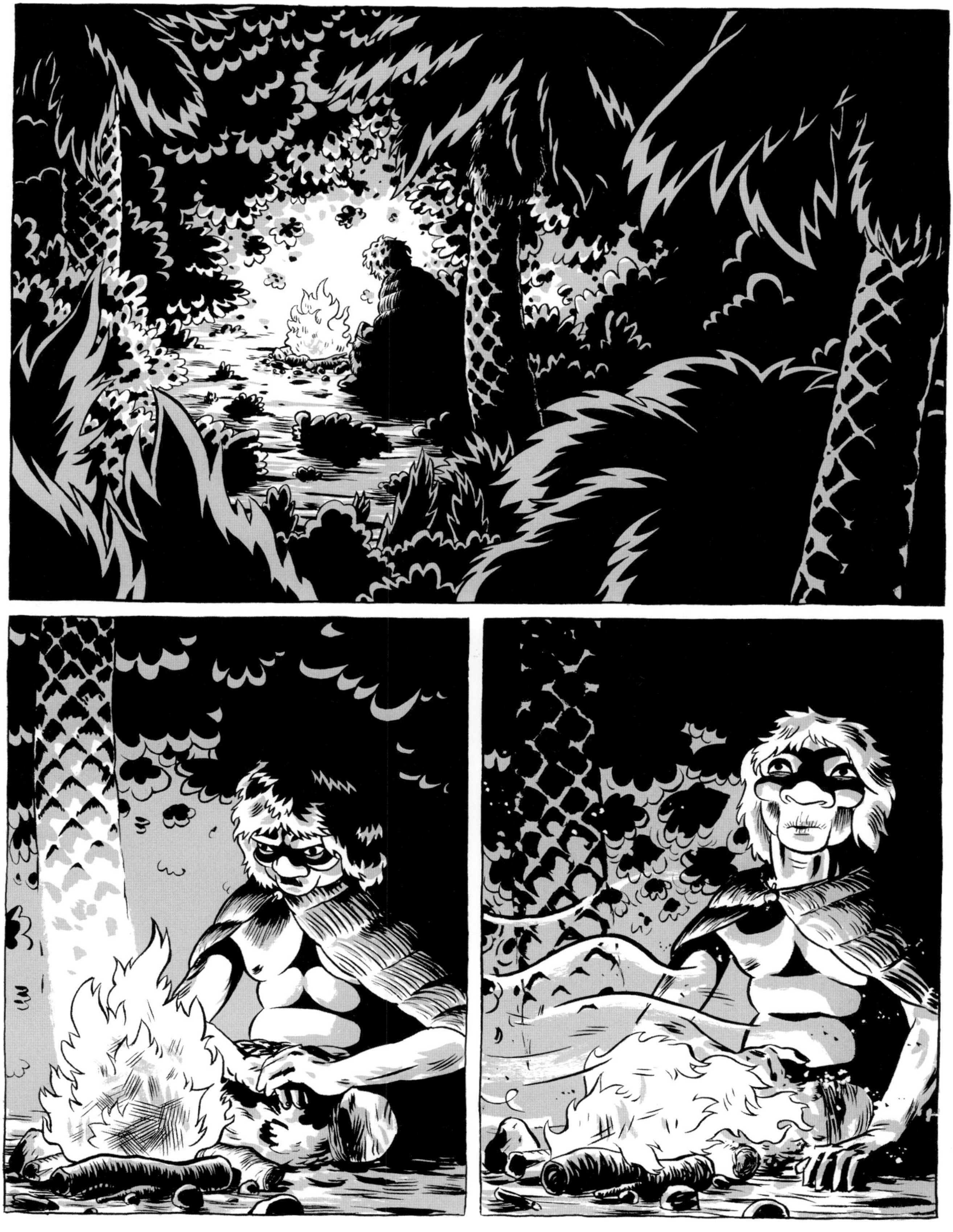

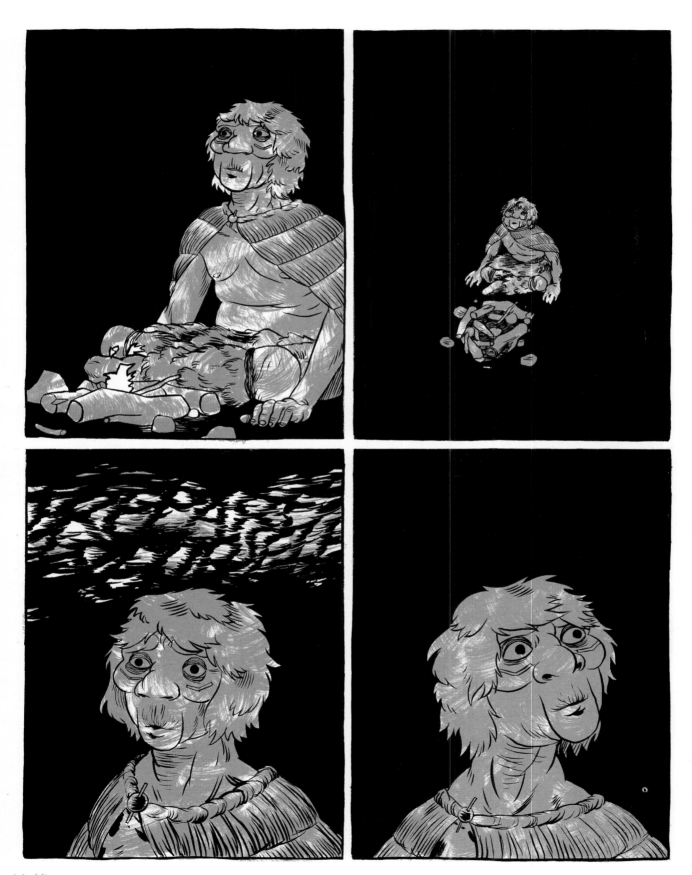

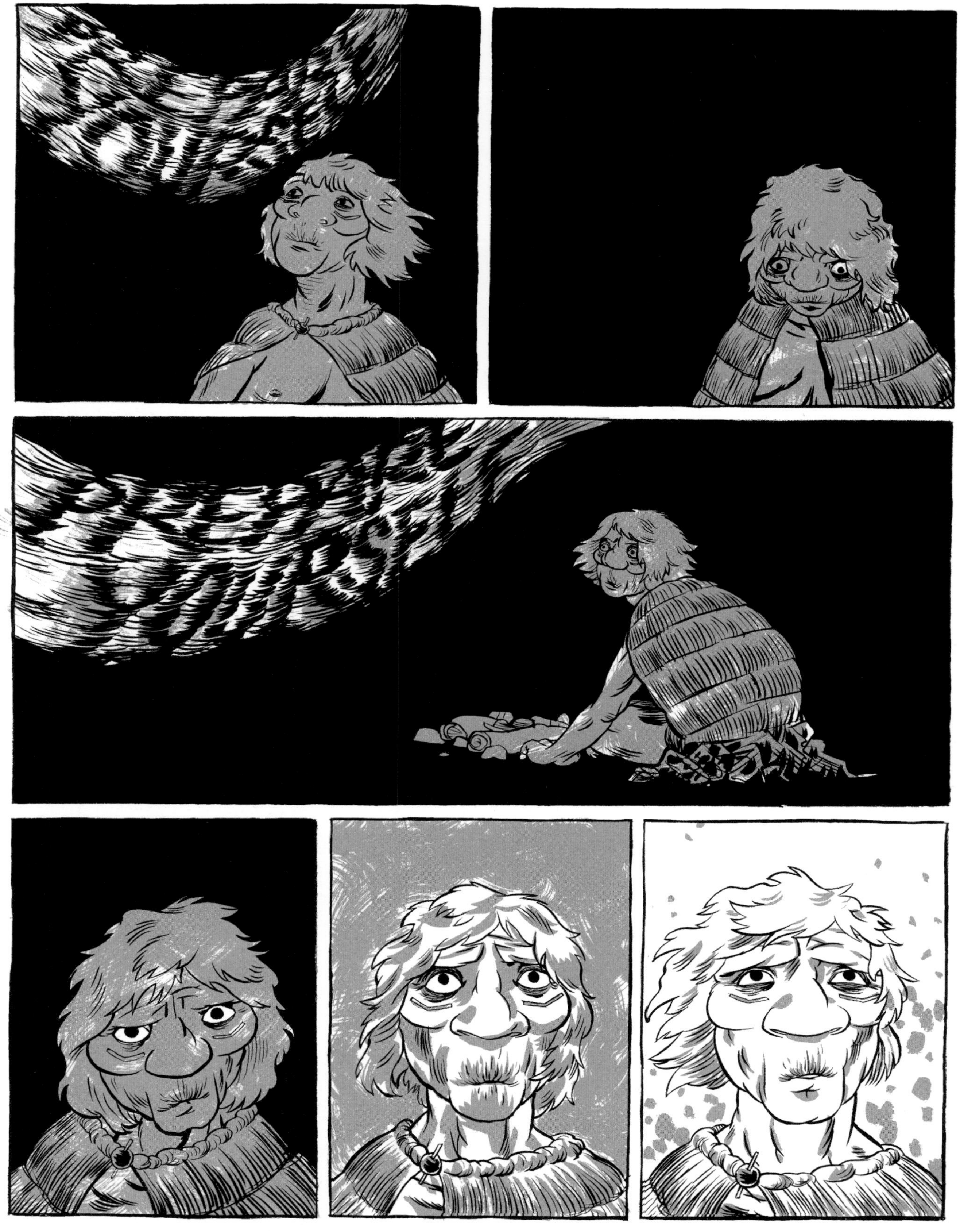

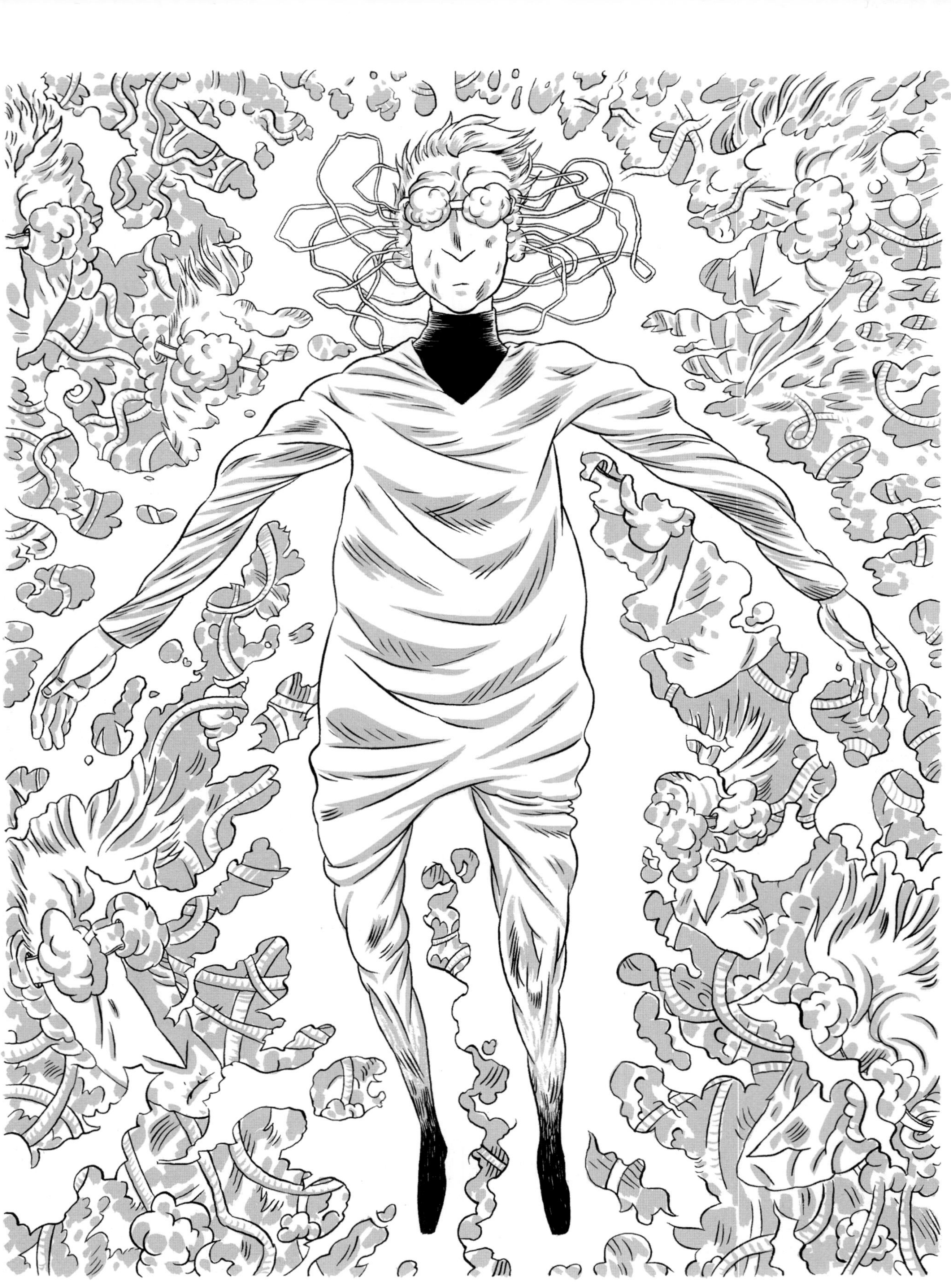

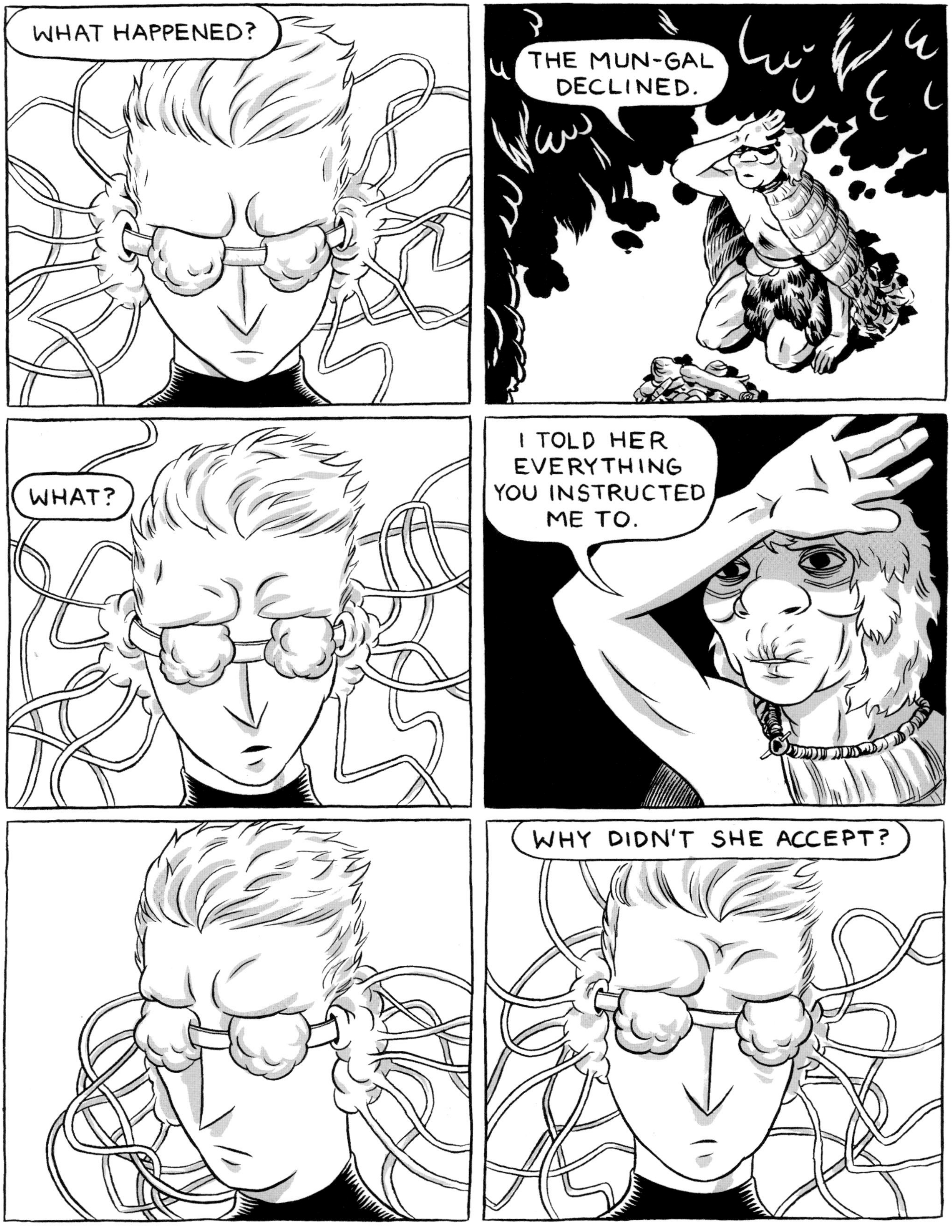
WHAT HAPPENED?
THE MUN-GAL DECLINED.
WHAT?
I TOLD HER EVERYTHING YOU INSTRUCTED ME TO.
WHY DIDN'T SHE ACCEPT?

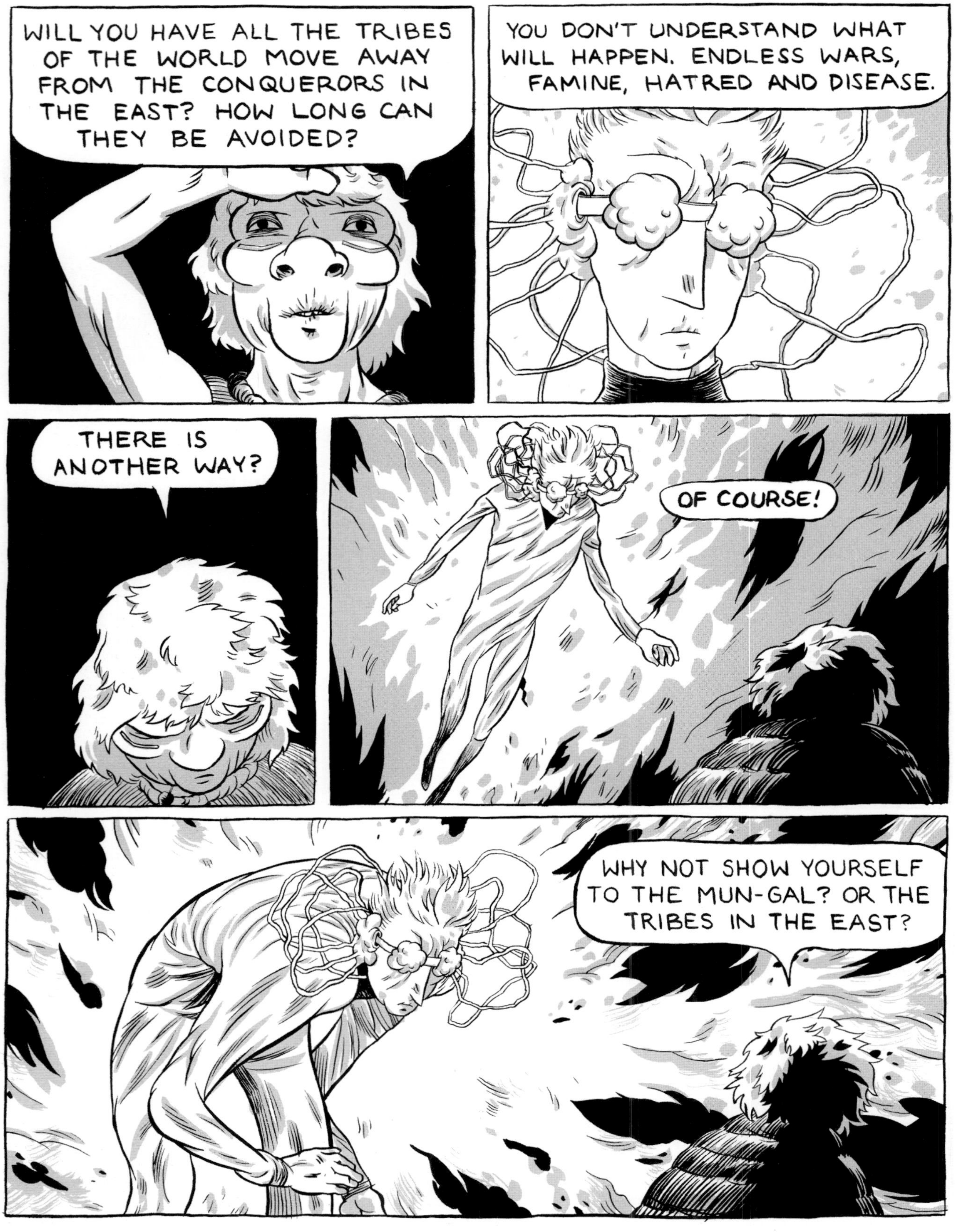
WILL YOU HAVE ALL THE TRIBES OF THE WORLD MOVE AWAY FROM THE CONQUERORS IN THE EAST? HOW LONG CAN THEY BE AVOIDED?
YOU DON'T UNDERSTAND WHAT WILL HAPPEN. ENDLESS WARS, FAMINE, HATRED AND DISEASE.
THERE IS ANOTHER WAY?
OF COURSE!
WHY NOT SHOW YOURSELF TO THE MUN-GAL? OR THE TRIBES IN THE EAST?

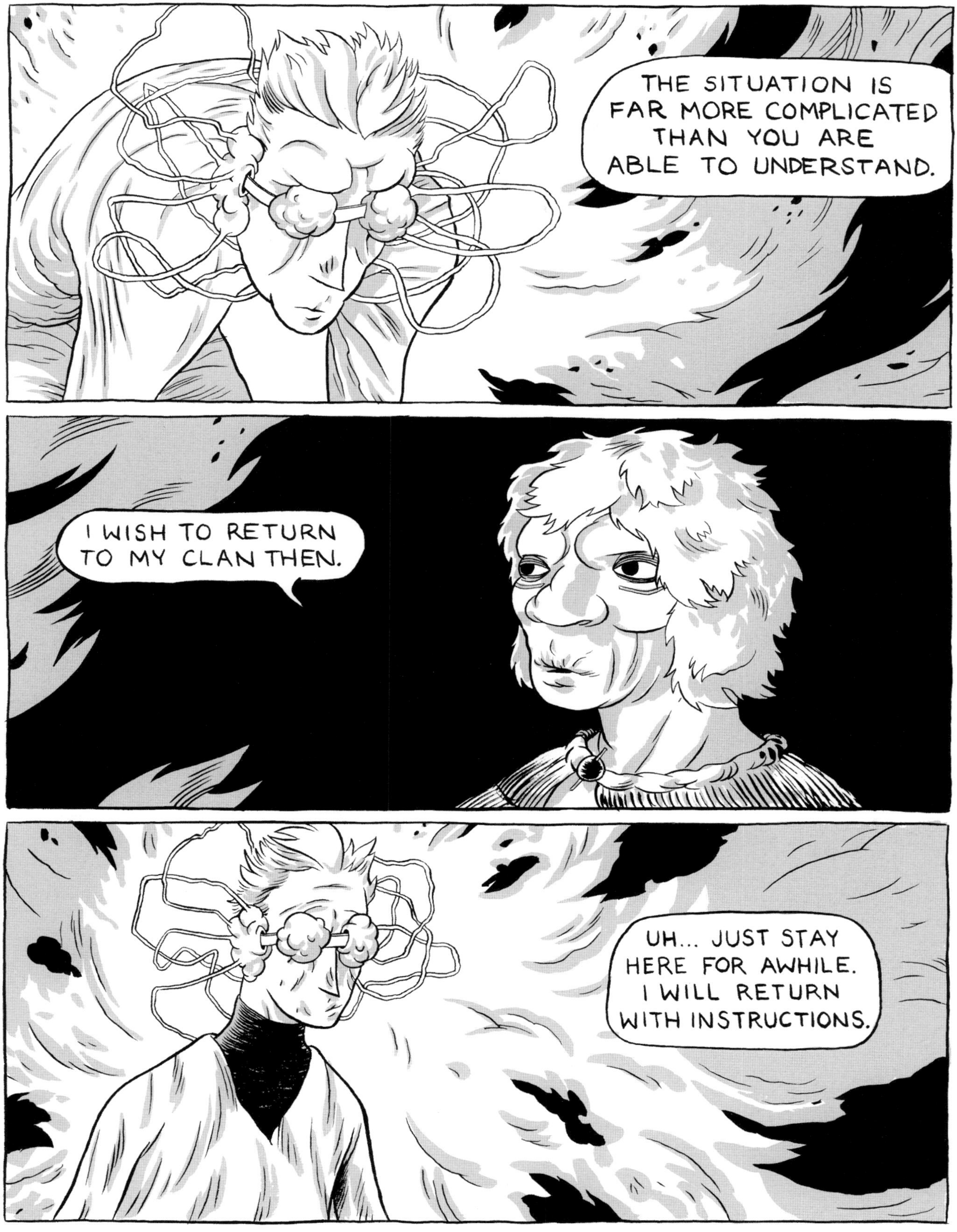
THE SITUATION IS FAR MORE COMPLICATED THAN YOU ARE ABLE TO UNDERSTAND.
I WISH TO RETURN TO MY CLAN THEN.
UH... JUST STAY HERE FOR AWHILE. I WILL RETURN WITH INSTRUCTIONS.

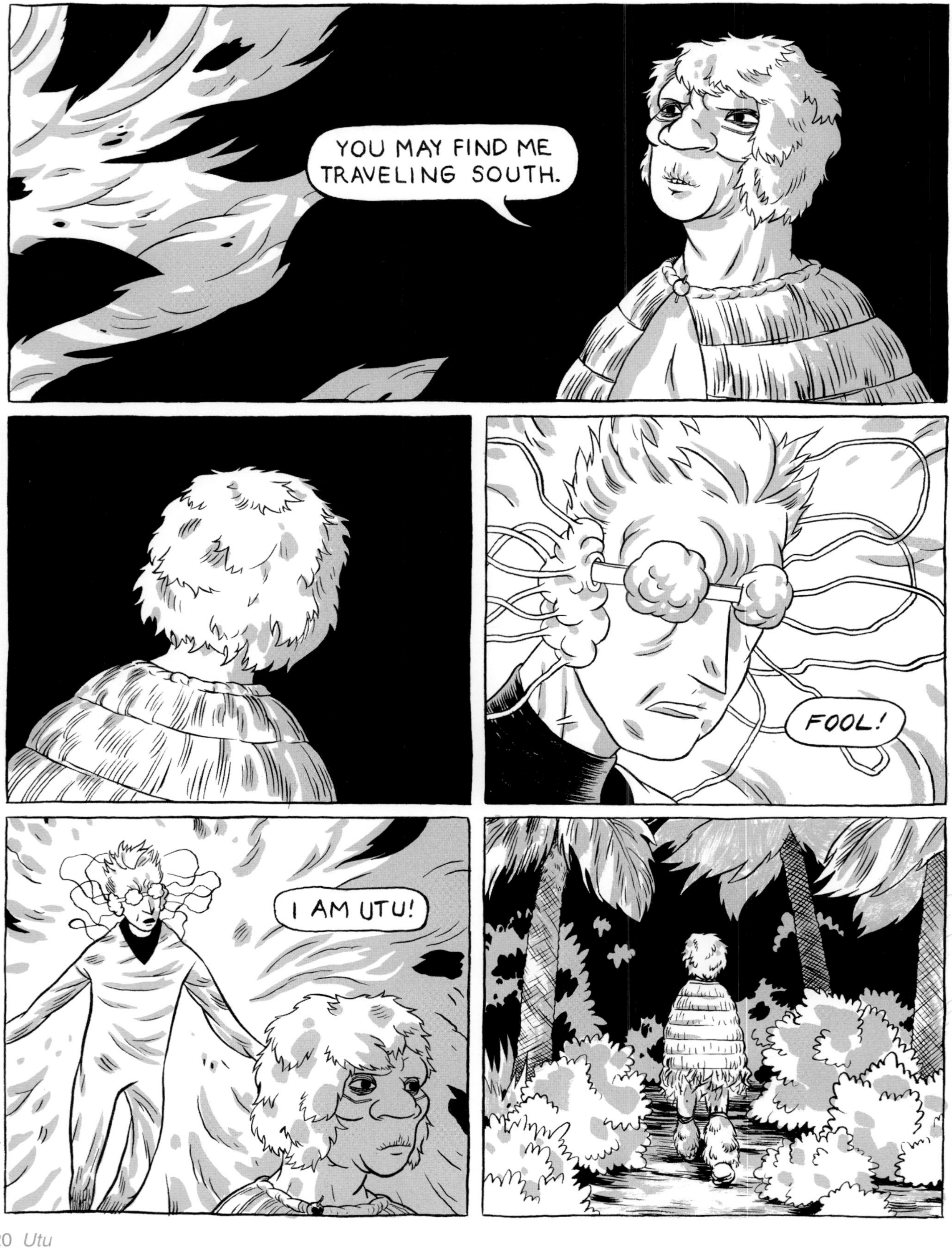
YOU MAY FIND ME TRAVELING SOUTH.
FOOL!
I AM UTU!

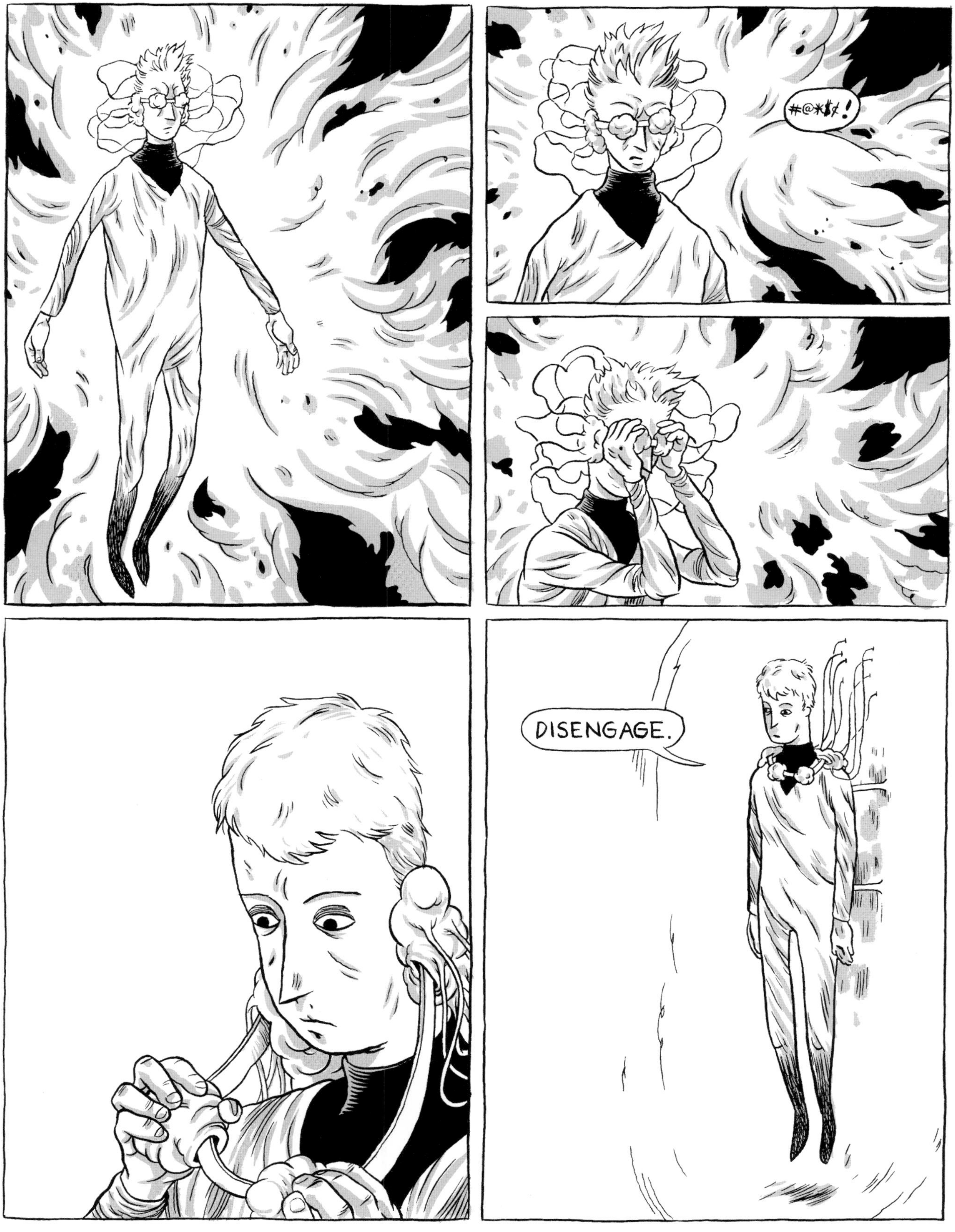

DISENGAGE.

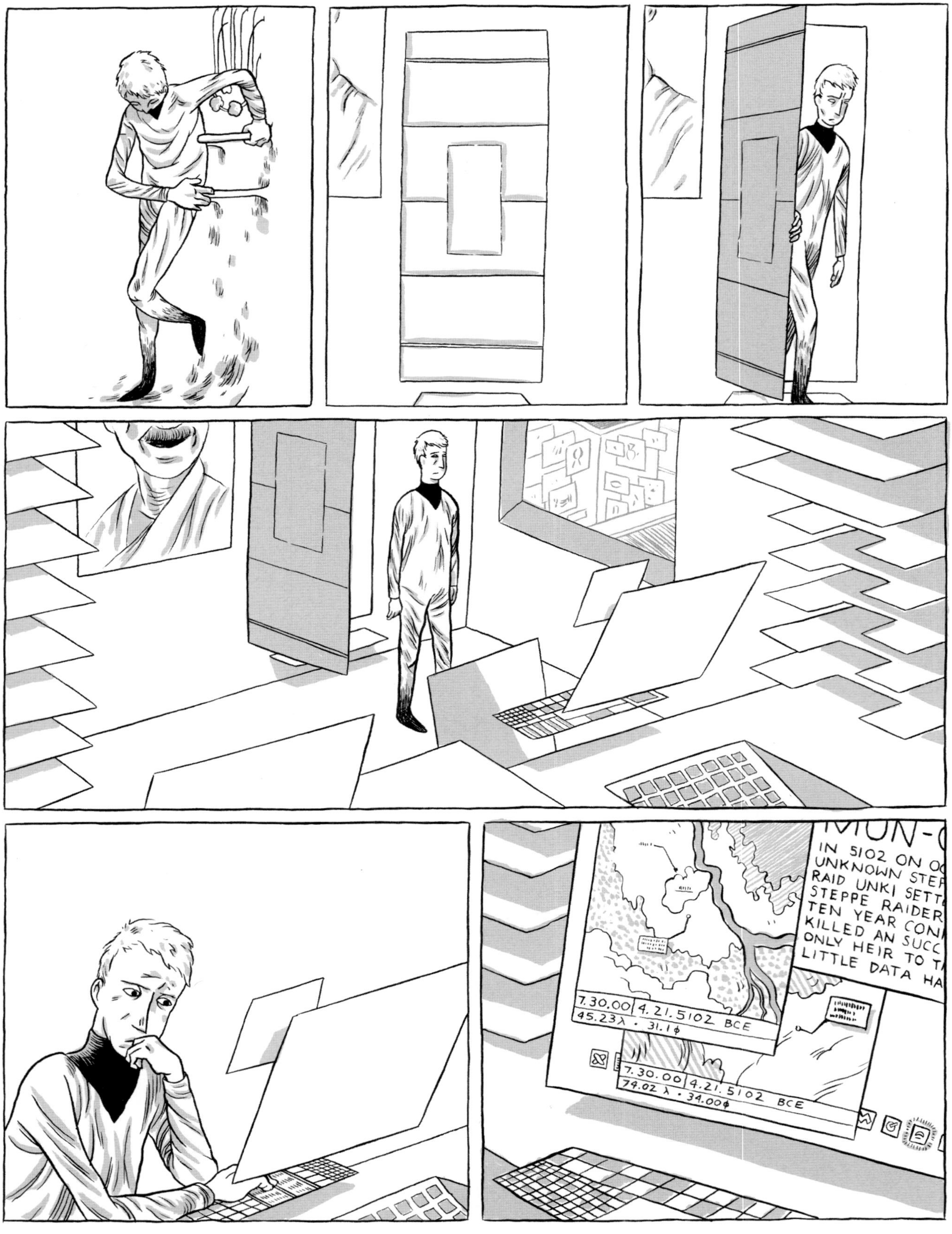
MUN-
IN 5102 ON O
UNKNOWN STE
RAID UNKI SETT
STEPPE RAIDER
TEN YEAR CON
KILLED AN SUCC
ONLY HEIR TO T
LITTLE DATA HA
7.30.00 4.21.5102 BCE
45.23λ • 31.1ϕ
7.30.00 4.21.5102 BCE
74.02 λ • 34.00ϕ

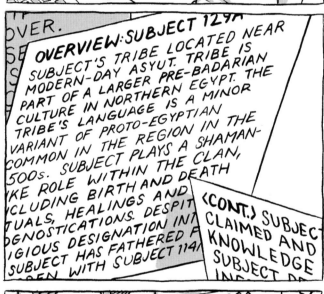

OVER.

OVERVIEW: SUBJECT 129A

SUBJECT'S TRIBE LOCATED NEAR MODERN-DAY ASYUT. TRIBE IS PART OF A LARGER PRE-BADARIAN CULTURE IN NORTHERN EGYPT. THE TRIBE'S LANGUAGE IS A MINOR VARIANT OF PROTO-EGYPTIAN COMMON IN THE REGION IN THE 500s. SUBJECT PLAYS A SHAMAN-[LI]KE ROLE WITHIN THE CLAN, [IN]CLUDING BIRTH AND DEATH [RI]TUALS, HEALINGS AND [PR]OGNOSTICATIONS. DESPIT[E] [REL]IGIOUS DESIGNATION [INT][O] SUBJECT HAS FATHERED [CHILD]REN WITH SUBJECT 114[A]

(CONT.) SUBJEC[T] CLAIMED AND KNOWLEDGE SUBJECT

[SUBJE]CT 129A HAS [WAR]NED AND DISPLAYED [KN]OWLEDGE OF FUTURE EVENTS. SUBJECT DESCRIBES RECEIVING INFORMATION IN DREAM FORM. THIS COULD BE THE RESULT OF THE ABNORMAL BRAIN ACTIVITY DESCRIBED IN REPORT X44. THERE ARE OTHER POSSIBLE EXPLANAT[IONS] FOR THE ABILITY TO... <CO[NT.)]

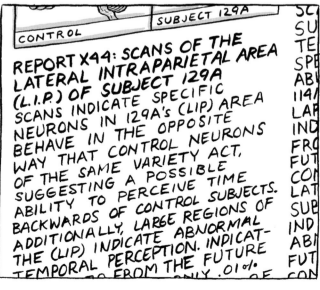

CONTROL	SUBJECT 129A

REPORT X44: SCANS OF THE LATERAL INTRAPARIETAL AREA (L.I.P.) OF SUBJECT 129A

SCANS INDICATE SPECIFIC NEURONS IN 129A's (LIP) AREA BEHAVE IN THE OPPOSITE WAY THAT CONTROL NEURONS OF THE SAME VARIETY ACT, SUGGESTING A POSSIBLE ABILITY TO PERCEIVE TIME BACKWARDS OF CONTROL SUBJECTS. ADDITIONALLY, LARGE REGIONS OF THE (LIP) INDICATE ABNORMAL TEMPORAL PERCEPTION. INDICAT[ING] [INT]O FROM THE FUTURE [T]O ONLY .01%.

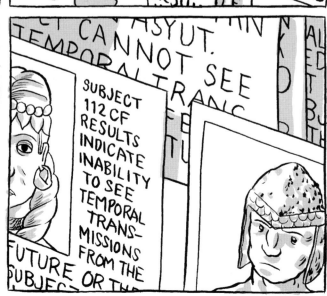

CANNOT SEE [ASYUT.] TEMPORAL TRANS[MISSIONS]

SUBJECT 112 CF RESULTS INDICATE INABILITY TO SEE TEMPORAL TRANS-MISSIONS FROM THE FUTURE OR TH[E]

23

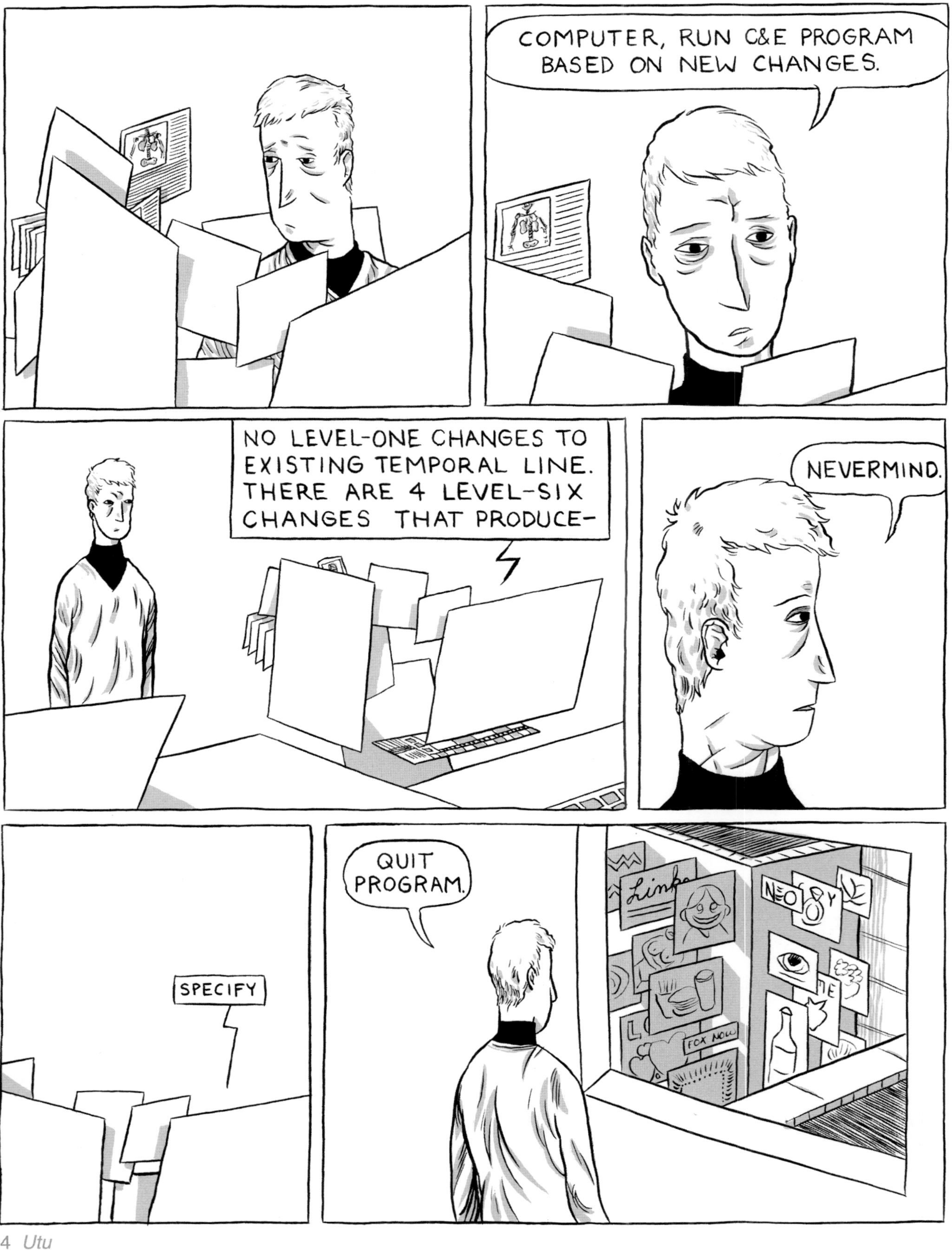
COMPUTER, RUN C&E PROGRAM BASED ON NEW CHANGES.
NO LEVEL-ONE CHANGES TO EXISTING TEMPORAL LINE. THERE ARE 4 LEVEL-SIX CHANGES THAT PRODUCE-
NEVERMIND.
SPECIFY
QUIT PROGRAM.

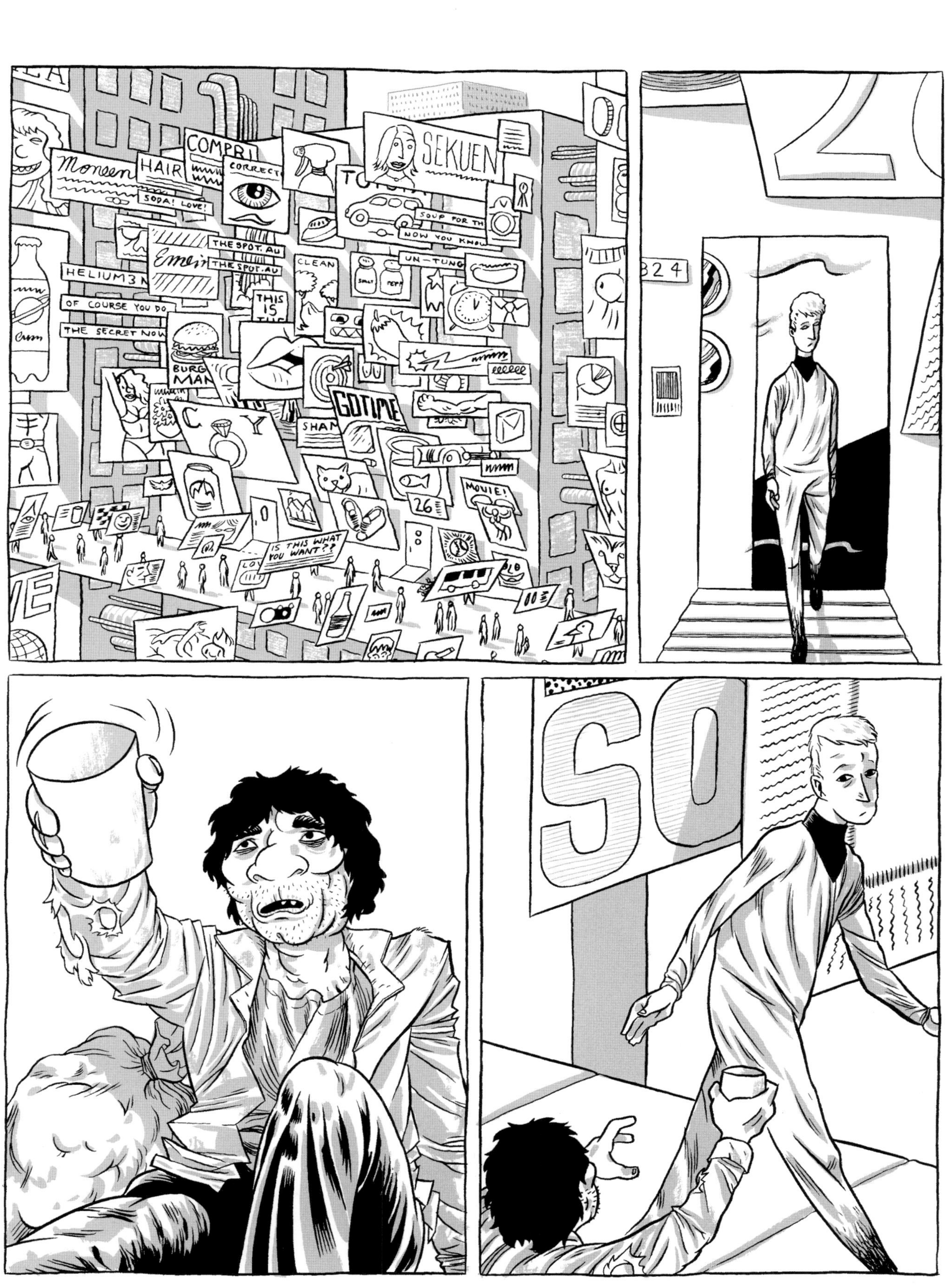
COMPRI
Moneen
HAIR
CORRECT
SEKUEN
SODA! LOVE!
SOUP FOR TH
NOW YOU KNOW
THE SPOT.AU
THE SPOT.AU
HELIUM3
OF COURSE YOU DO
THE SECRET NOW
CLEAN
UN-TUNG
THIS IS
GOTIME
SHAM
MOVIE!
26
IS THIS WHAT YOU WANT??
324
SO

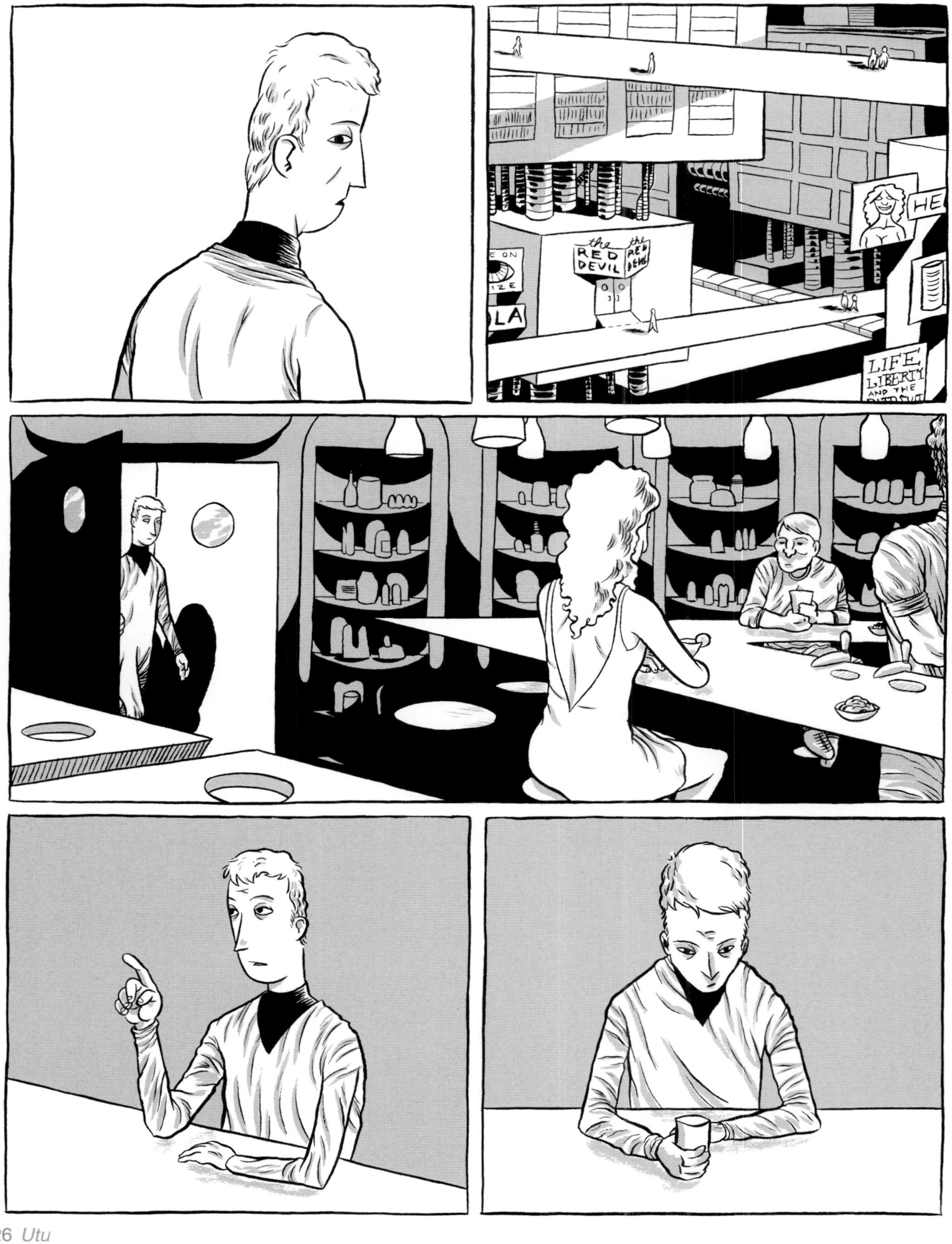
the RED DEVIL
the RED DEVIL
LIFE, LIBERTY AND THE

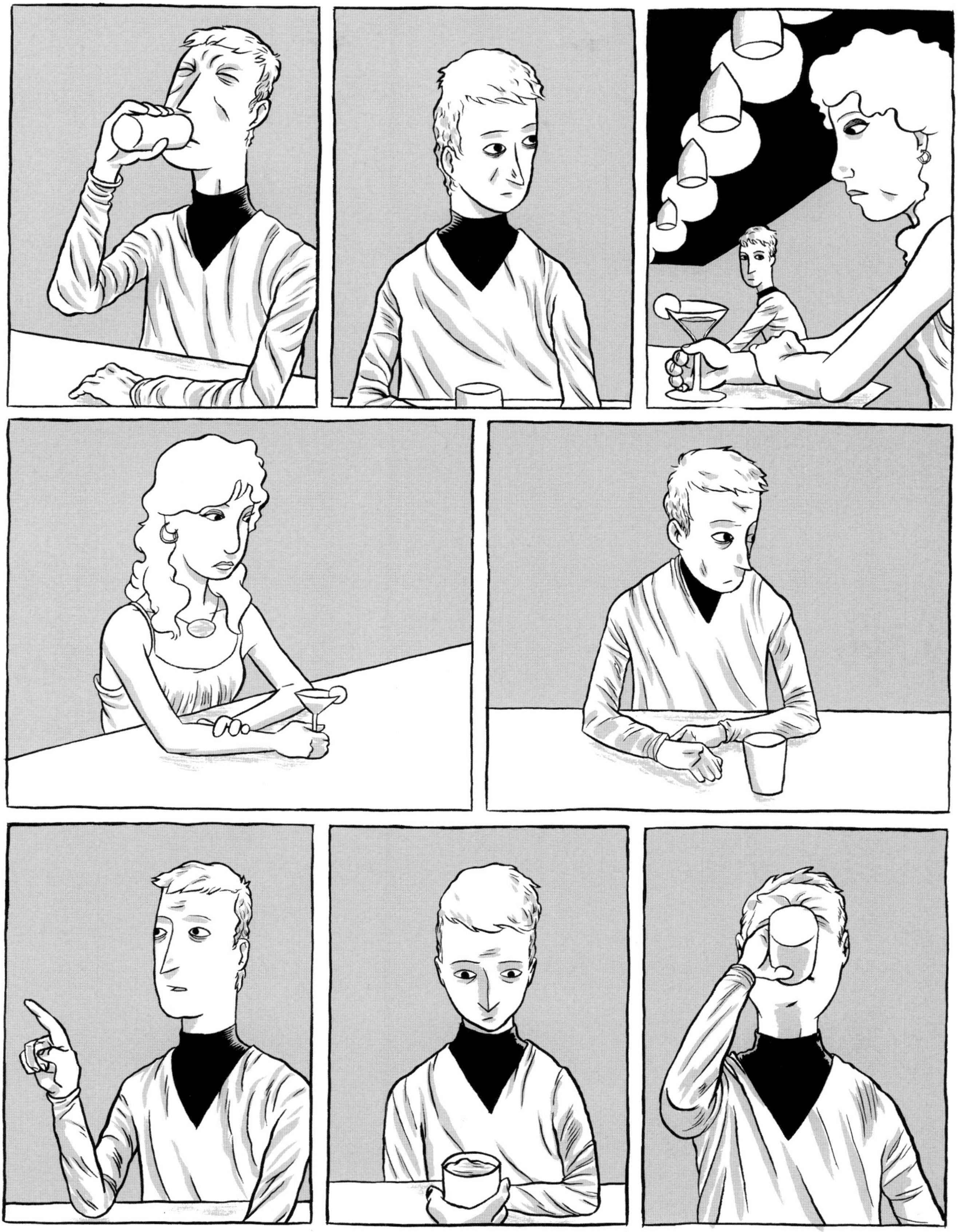

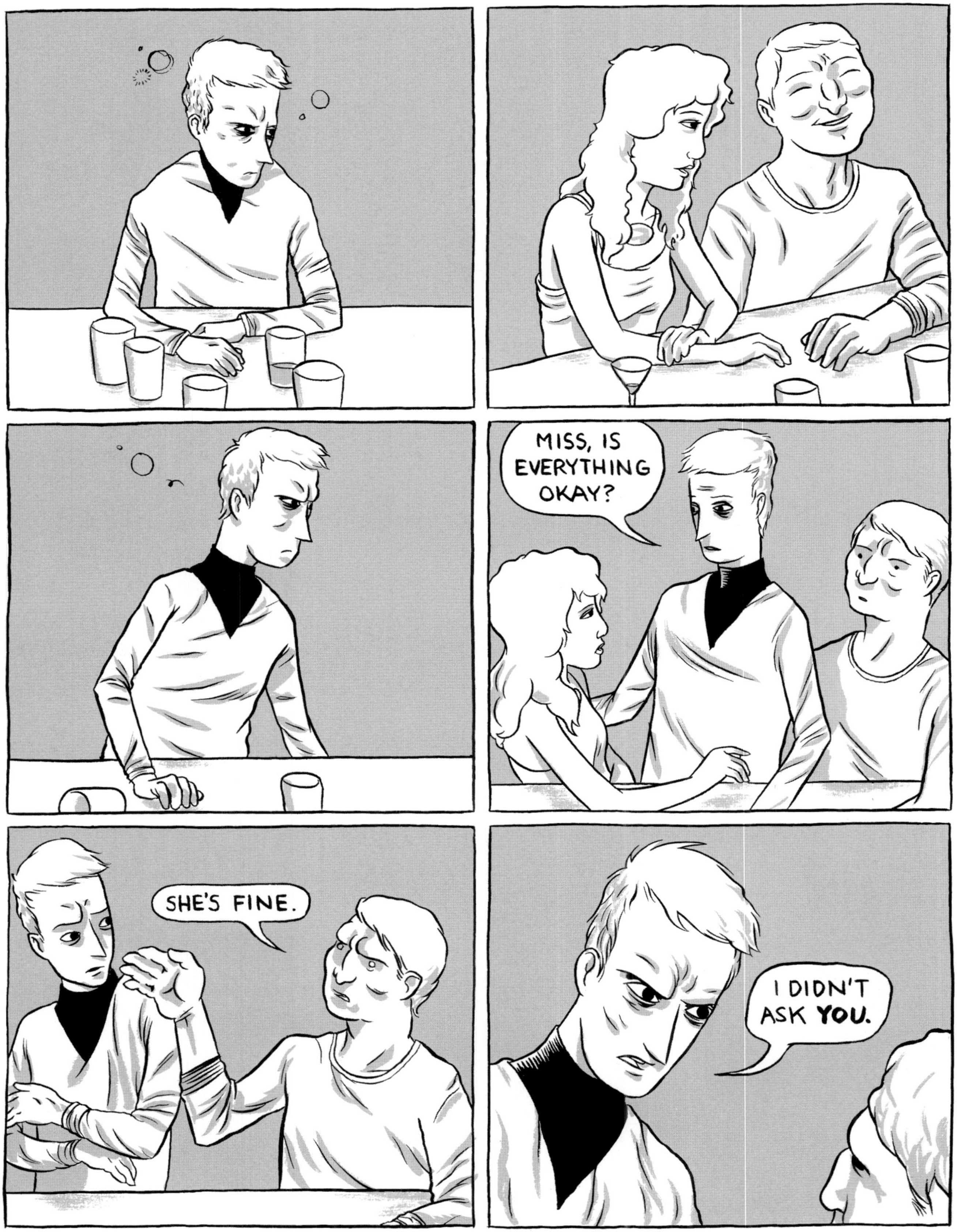
MISS, IS EVERYTHING OKAY?
SHE'S FINE.
I DIDN'T ASK **YOU**.

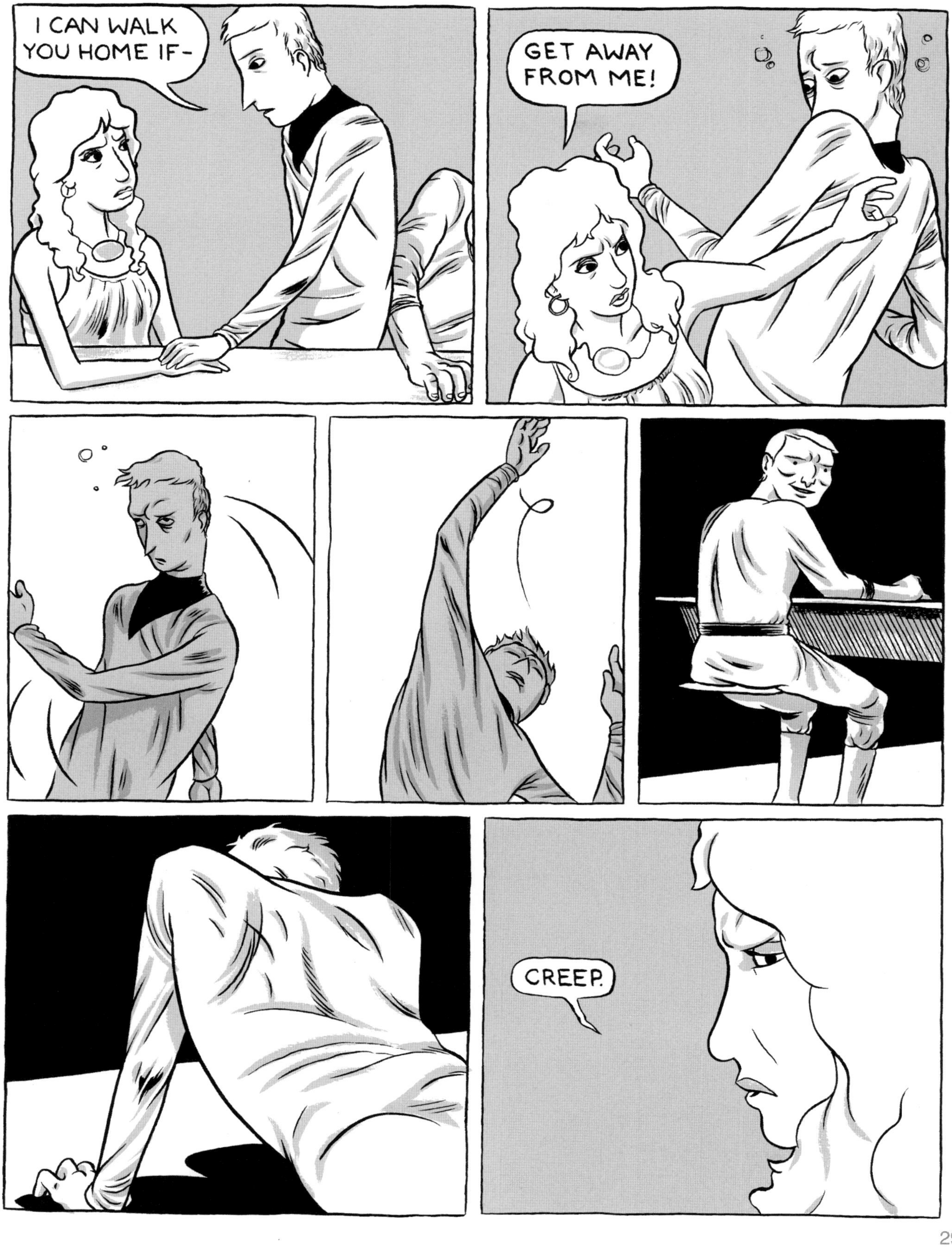
I CAN WALK YOU HOME IF-
GET AWAY FROM ME!
CREEP.

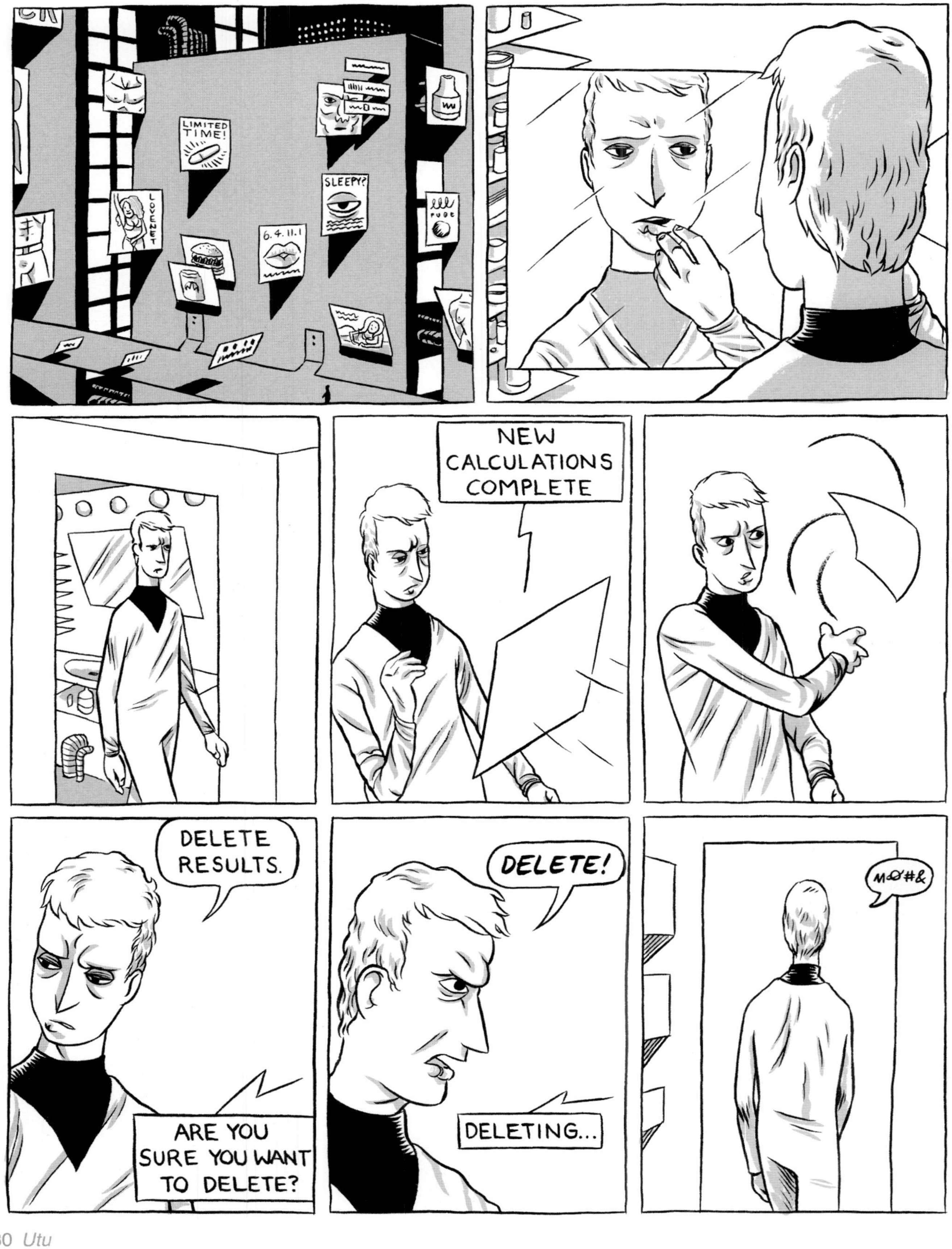
LIMITED TIME!
SLEEPY?
6.4.11.1
LOVENET
NEW CALCULATIONS COMPLETE
DELETE RESULTS.
ARE YOU SURE YOU WANT TO DELETE?
DELETE!
DELETING...

TURN OFF THE LIGHTS.
THE END

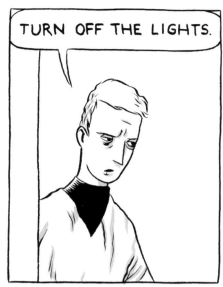

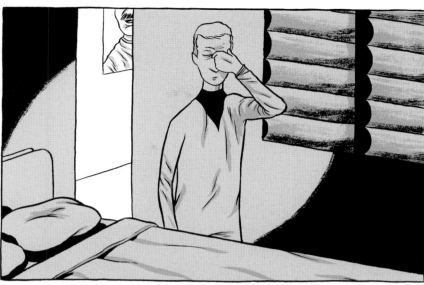

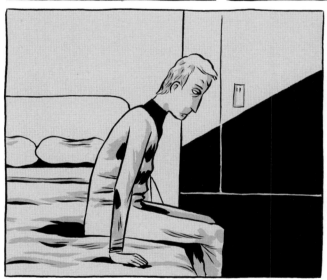

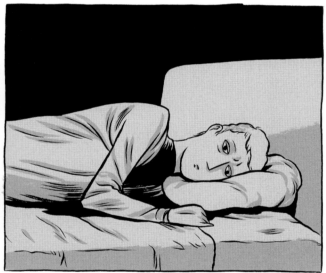

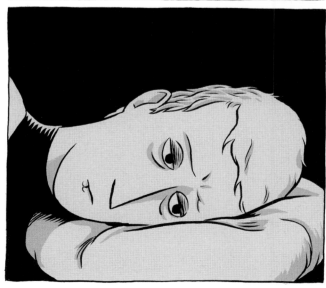

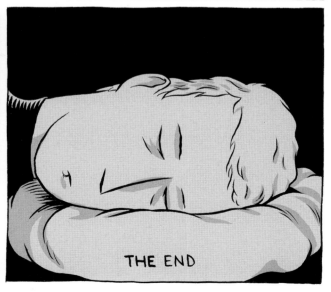

THE HORSEHEAD NEBULA IS GORGEOUS.
THE NEXT DAY
(ZOOM)

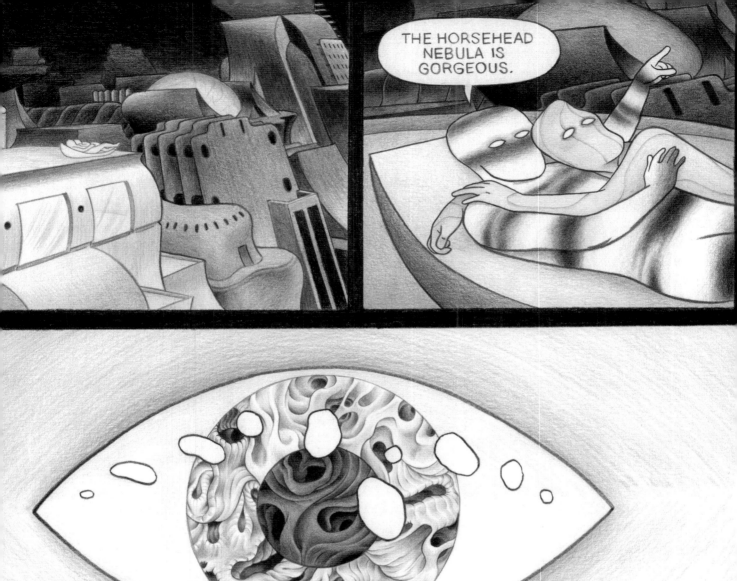

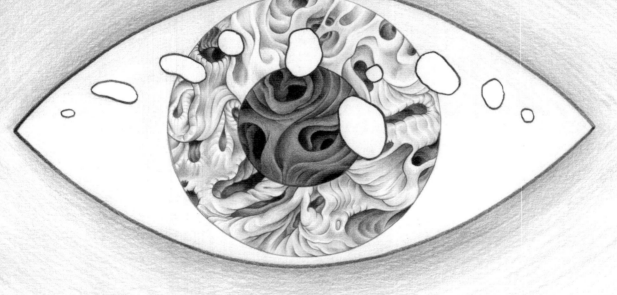

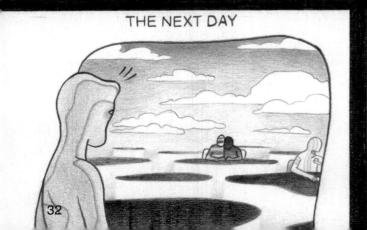

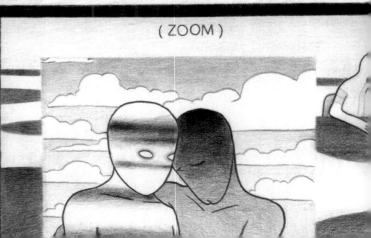

I DON'T SEE IT...
ADJUST YOUR VISION TO DETECT INFRARED.
OK-
BLINK
BLINK

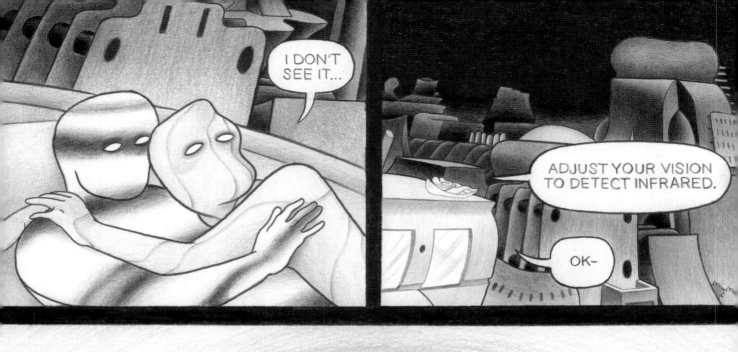

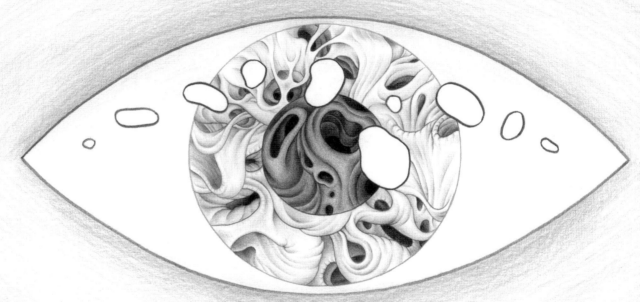

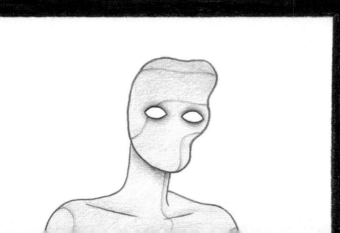

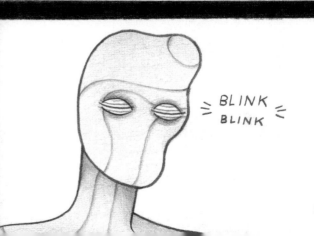

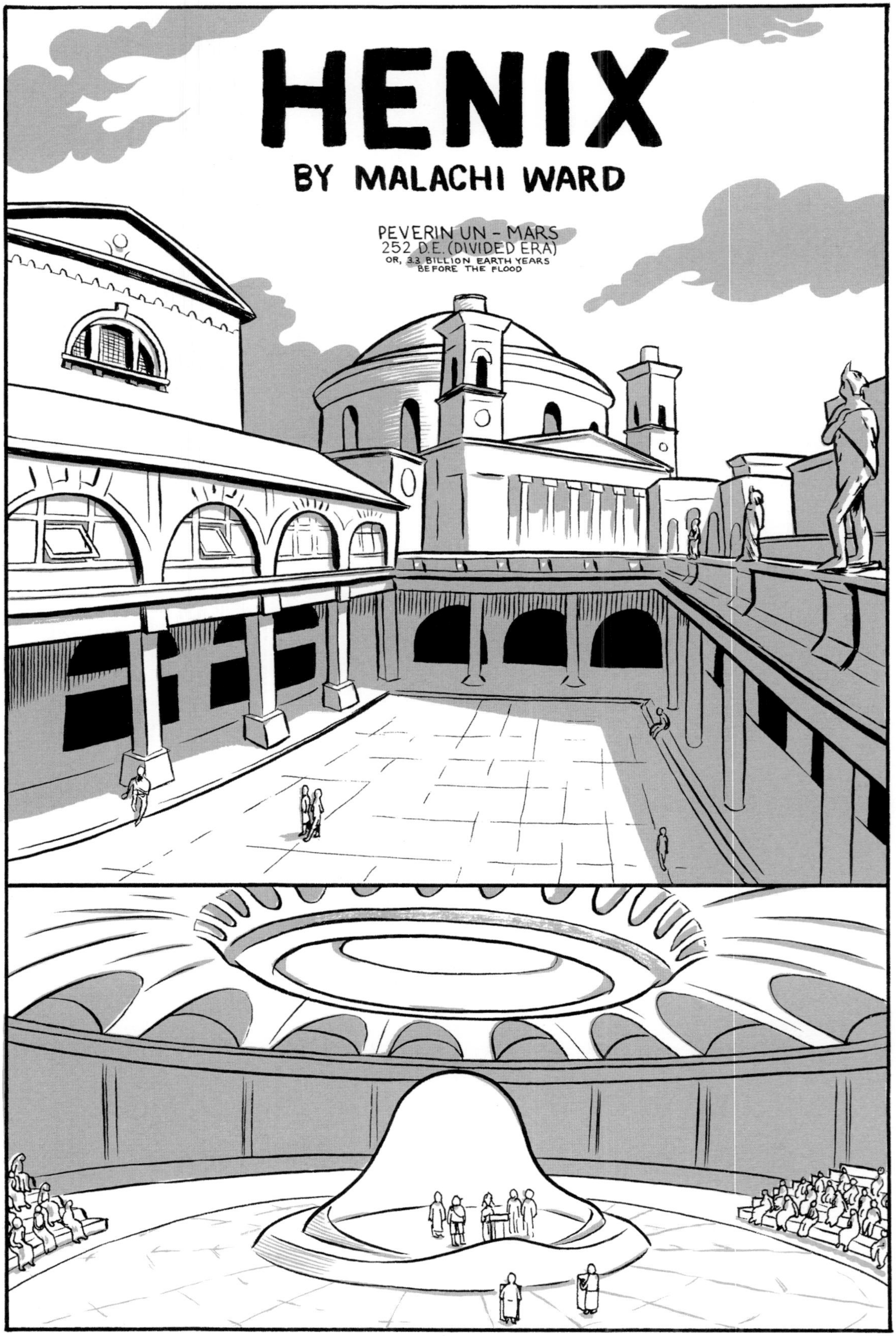
HENIX
BY MALACHI WARD
PEVERIN UN - MARS
252 D.E. (DIVIDED ERA)
OR, 3.3 BILLION EARTH YEARS BEFORE THE FLOOD

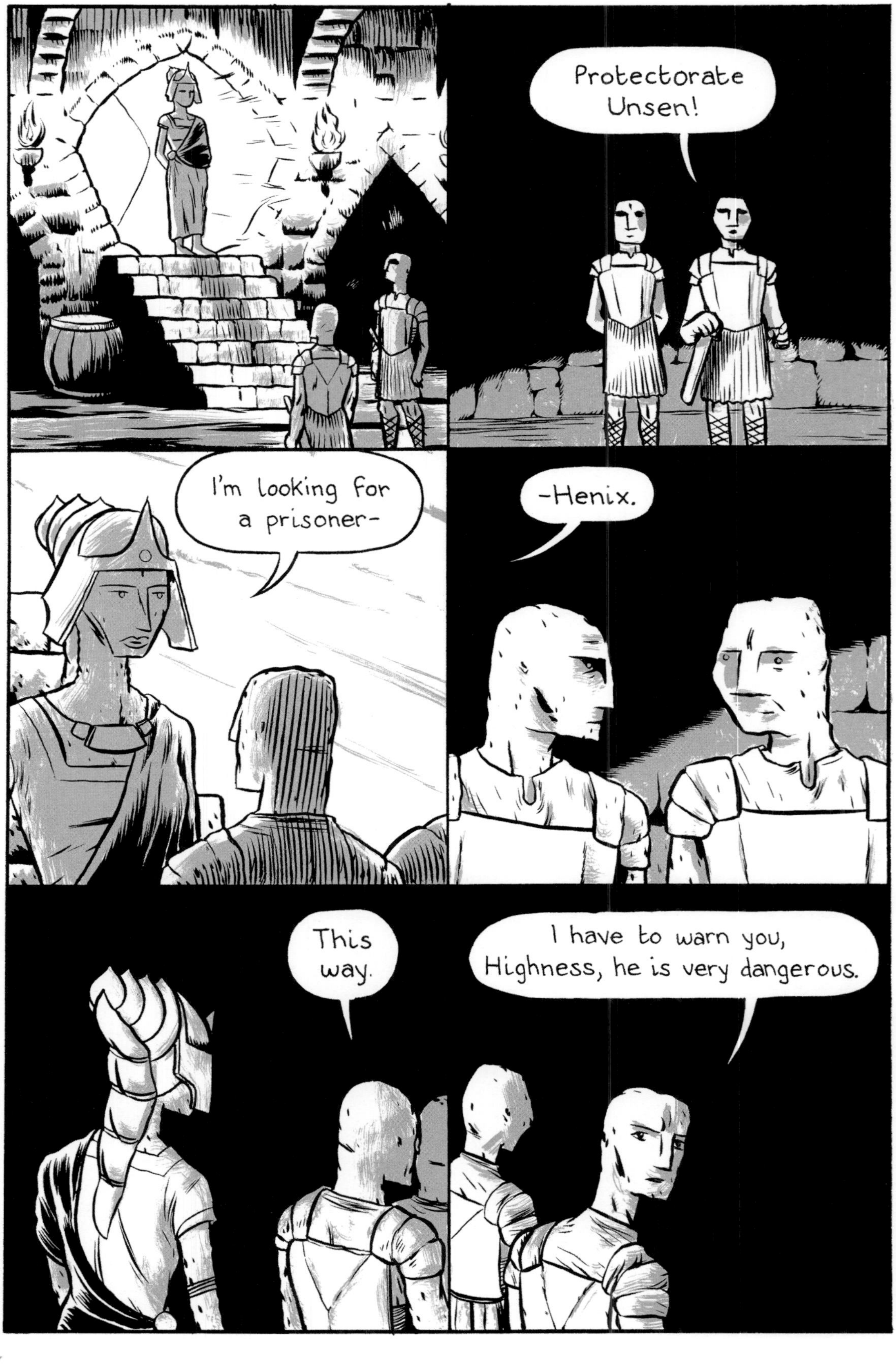

Protectorate Unsen!
I'm looking for a prisoner-
-Henix.
This way.
I have to warn you, Highness, he is very dangerous.

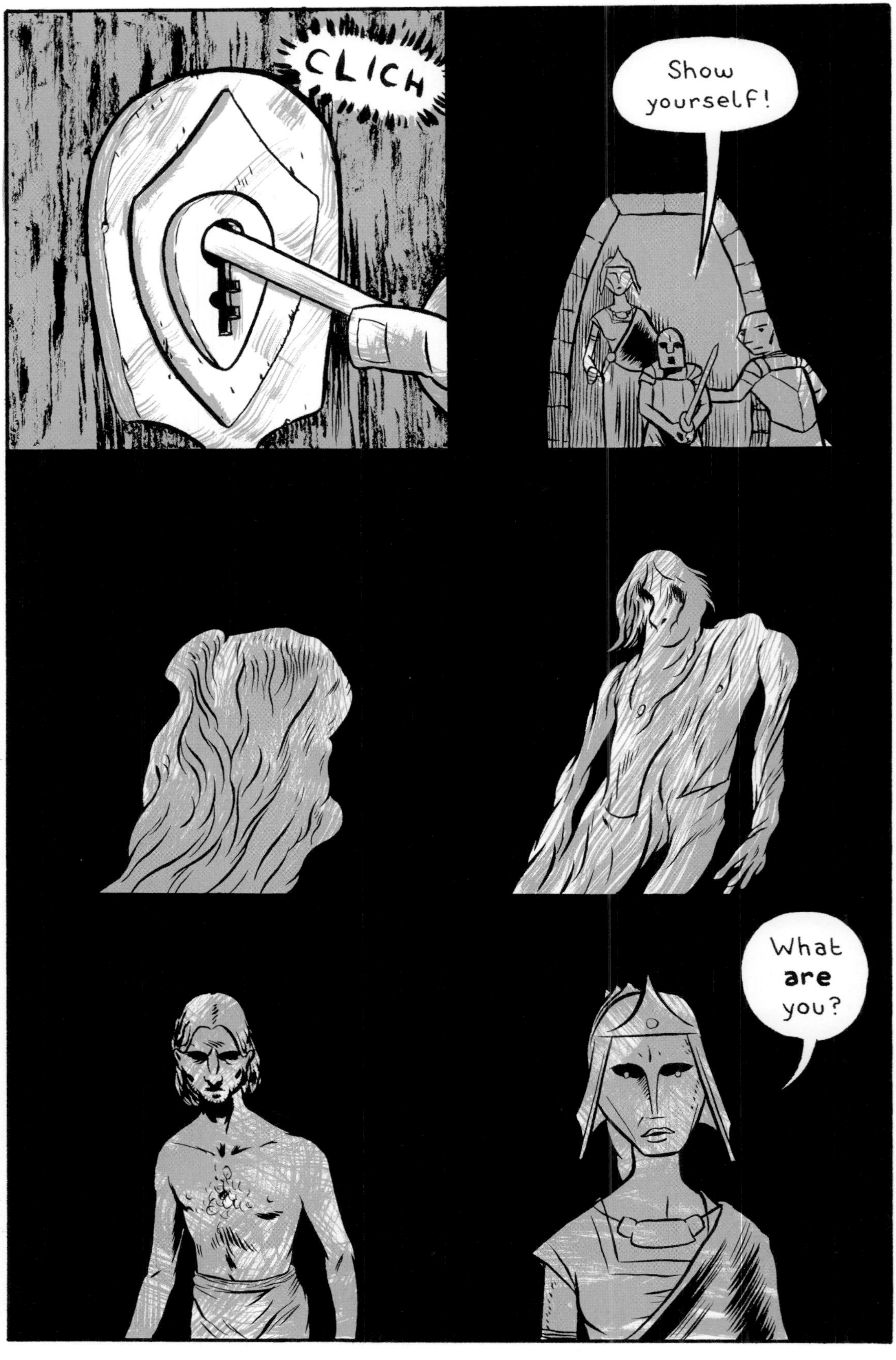
CLICH
Show yourself!
What **are** you?

41

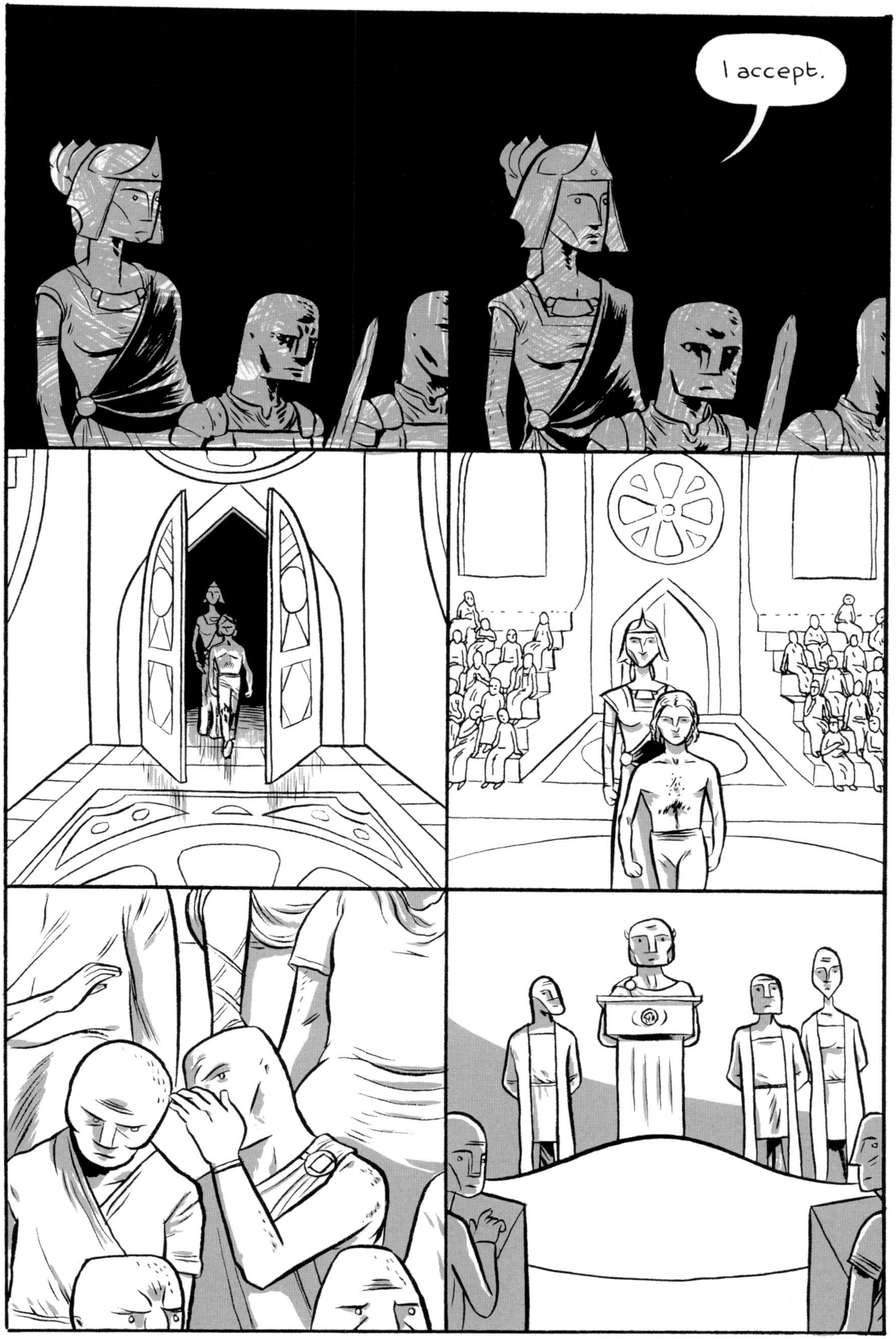
I accept.

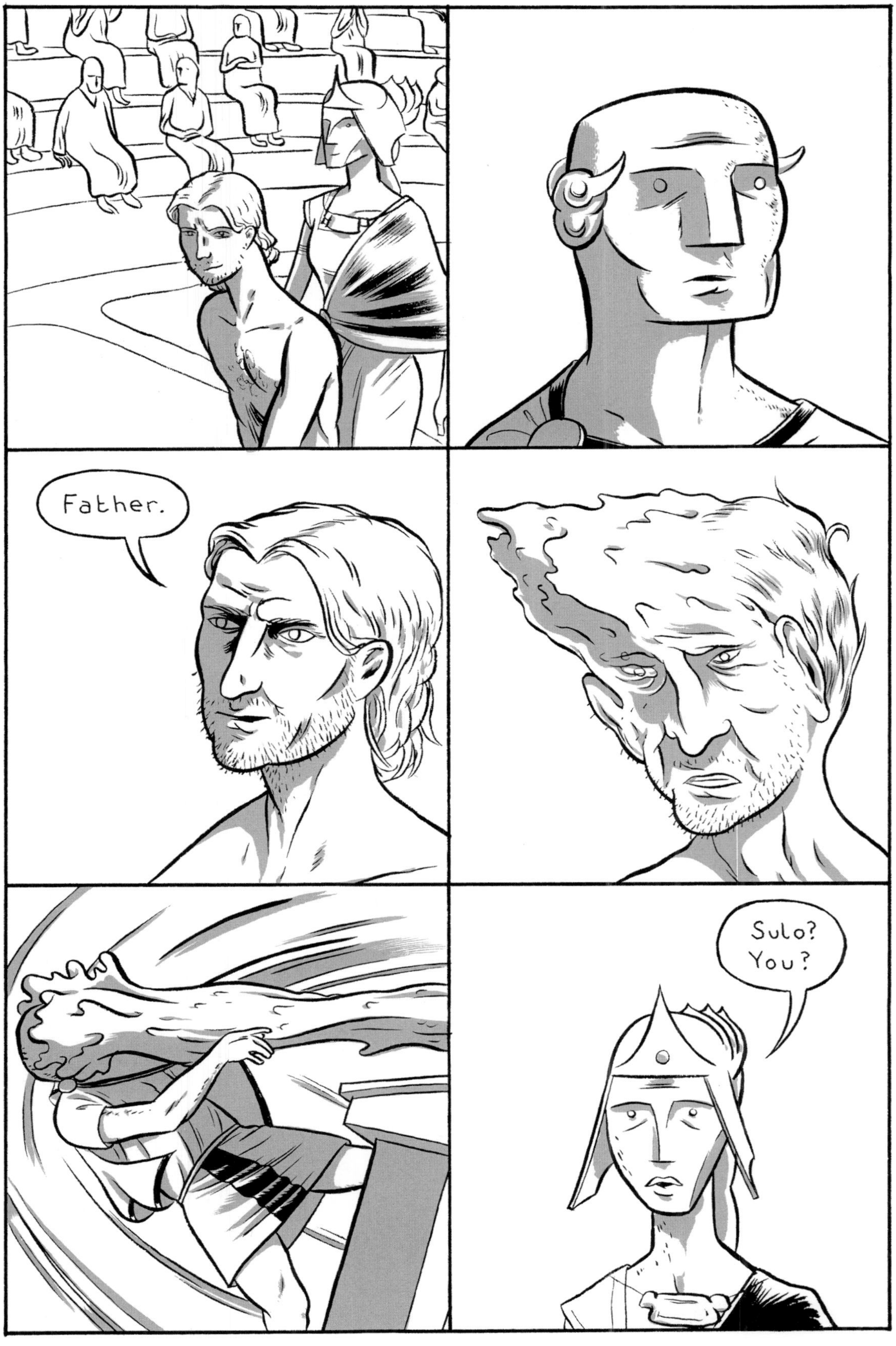
Father.
Sulo? You?

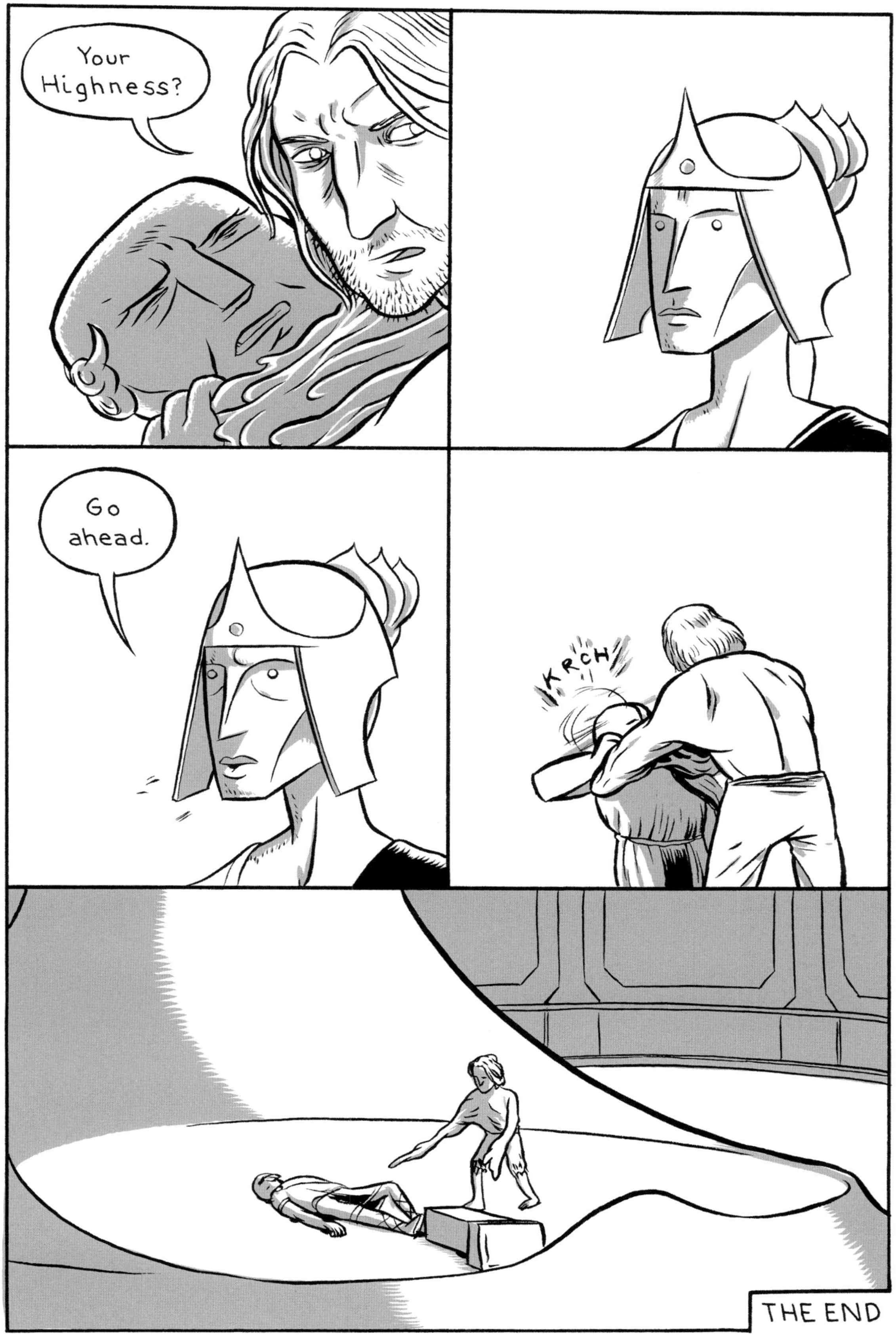
Your Highness?
Go ahead.
KRCH
THE END

Divination
by Malachi Ward

NEGATIVE SPACE

MALACHI · 2012

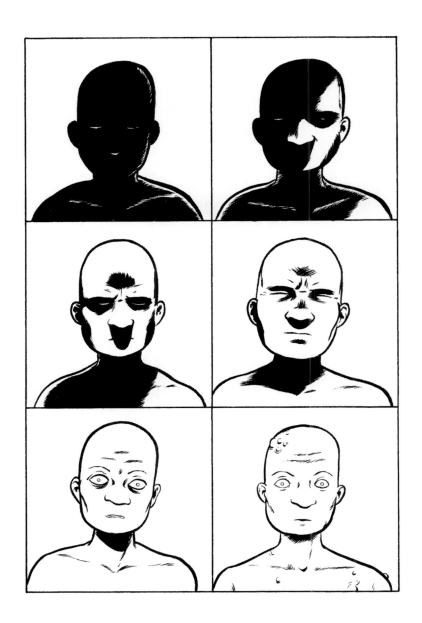

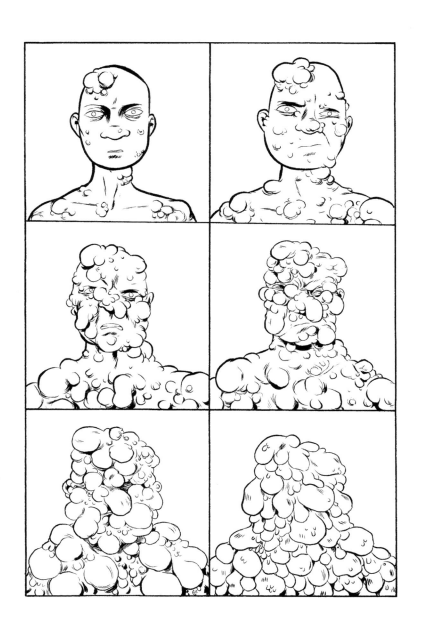

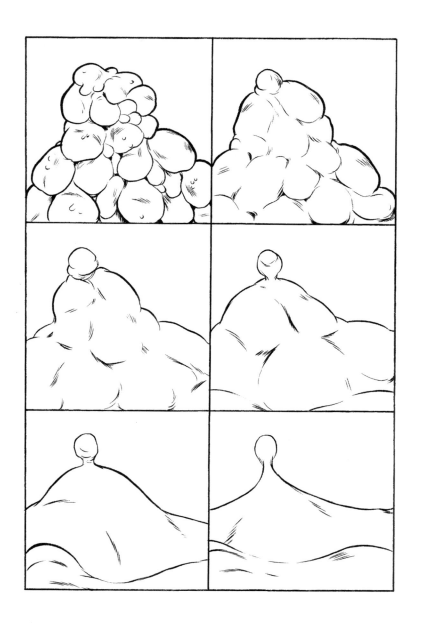

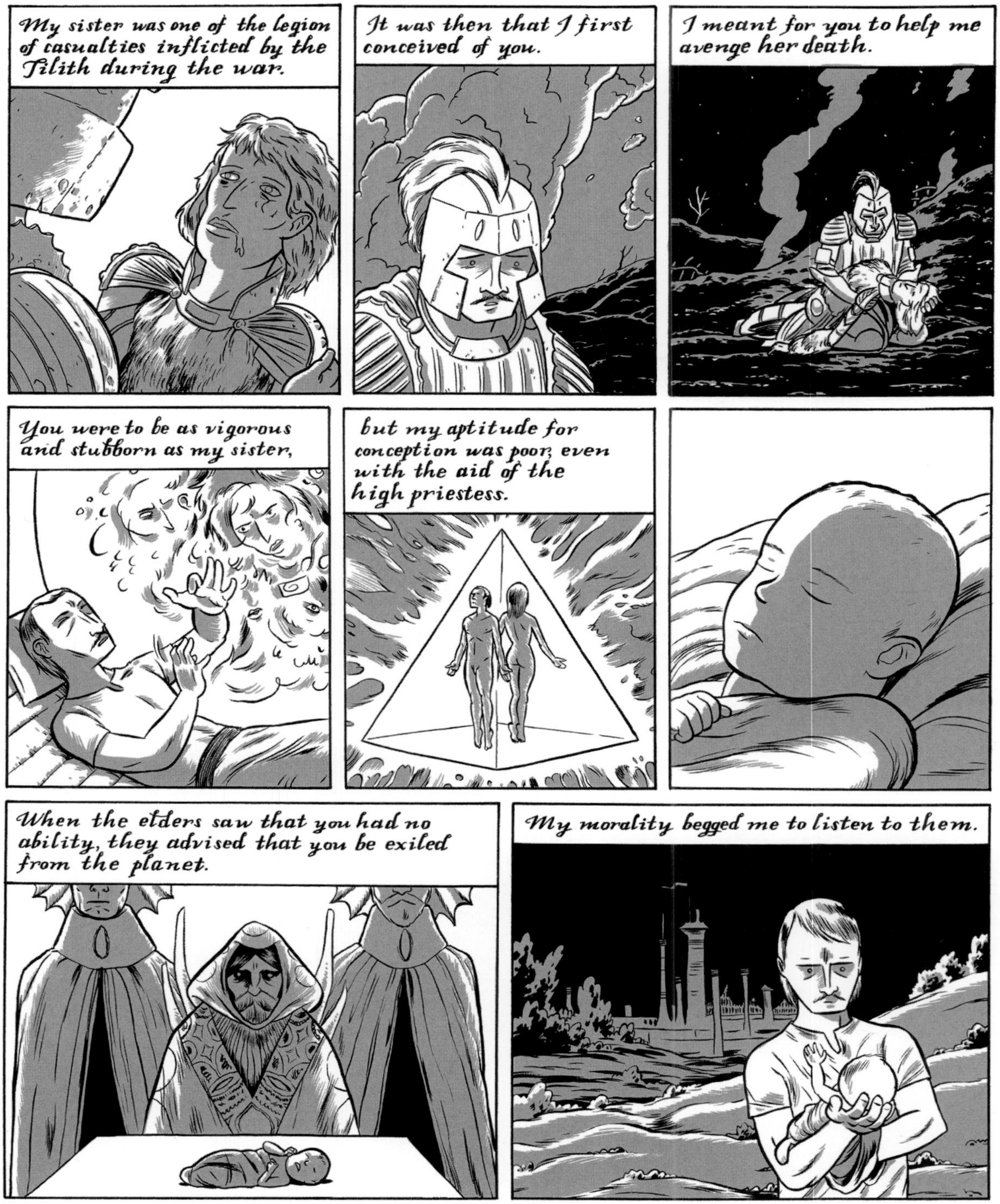
My sister was one of the legion of casualties inflicted by the Tilith during the war.
It was then that I first conceived of you.
I meant for you to help me avenge her death.
You were to be as vigorous and stubborn as my sister,
but my aptitude for conception was poor, even with the aid of the high priestess.
When the elders saw that you had no ability, they advised that you be exiled from the planet.
My morality begged me to listen to them.

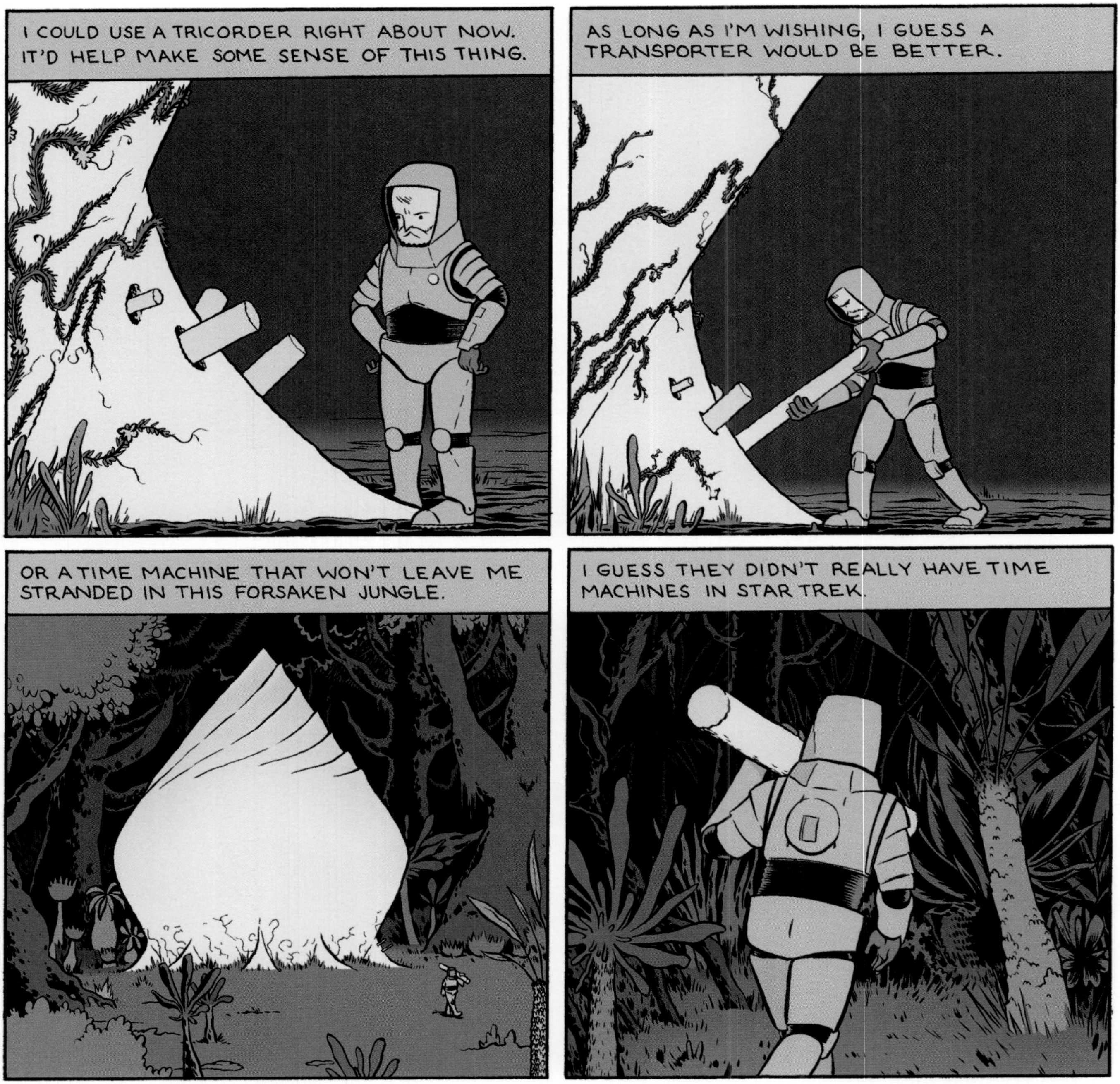
I COULD USE A TRICORDER RIGHT ABOUT NOW. IT'D HELP MAKE SOME SENSE OF THIS THING.
AS LONG AS I'M WISHING, I GUESS A TRANSPORTER WOULD BE BETTER.
OR A TIME MACHINE THAT WON'T LEAVE ME STRANDED IN THIS FORSAKEN JUNGLE.
I GUESS THEY DIDN'T REALLY HAVE TIME MACHINES IN STAR TREK.

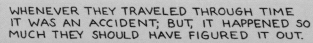

WE BEAT YOU THERE, RODDENBERRY.

WHENEVER THEY TRAVELED THROUGH TIME IT WAS AN ACCIDENT; BUT, IT HAPPENED SO MUCH THEY SHOULD HAVE FIGURED IT OUT.

WHAT DID KIRK DO IN "THE VOYAGE HOME?" GO AROUND THE SUN REALLY FAST? STUPID.

OF COURSE—IN DEEP SPACE NINE—ANY TIME THEY WANTED TO TIME-TRAVEL, THE "ORB OF TIME" SENT THEM.

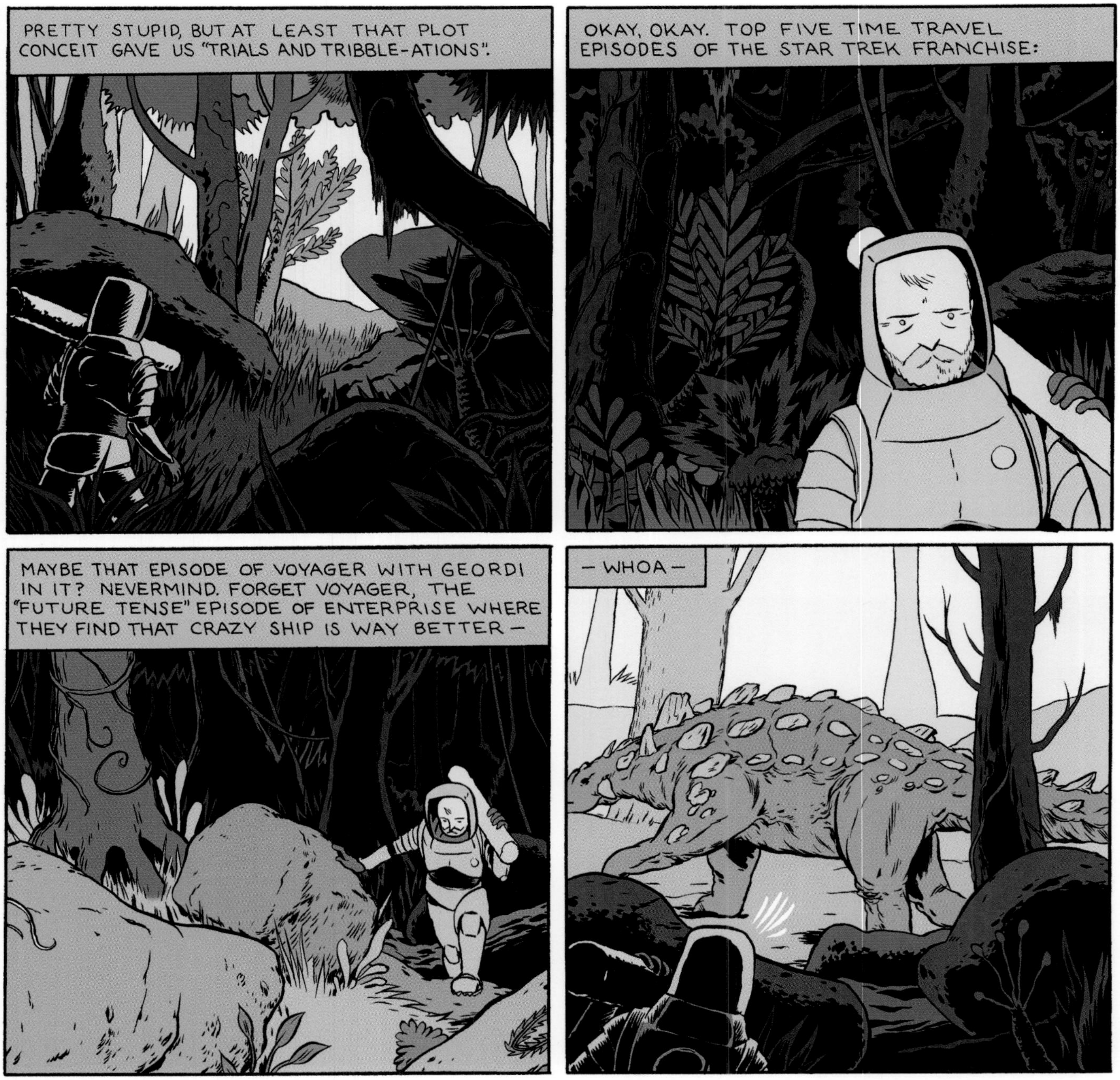
PRETTY STUPID, BUT AT LEAST THAT PLOT CONCEIT GAVE US "TRIALS AND TRIBBLE-ATIONS".
OKAY, OKAY. TOP FIVE TIME TRAVEL EPISODES OF THE STAR TREK FRANCHISE:
MAYBE THAT EPISODE OF VOYAGER WITH GEORDI IN IT? NEVERMIND. FORGET VOYAGER, THE "FUTURE TENSE" EPISODE OF ENTERPRISE WHERE THEY FIND THAT CRAZY SHIP IS WAY BETTER—
—WHOA—

VOYAGER WAS SUCH A CRAPPY SHOW.

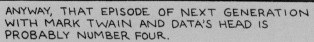

ANYWAY, THAT EPISODE OF NEXT GENERATION WITH MARK TWAIN AND DATA'S HEAD IS PROBABLY NUMBER FOUR.

NEXT GENERATION'S "ALL GOOD THINGS," I'D PUT THAT AT NUMBER THREE.

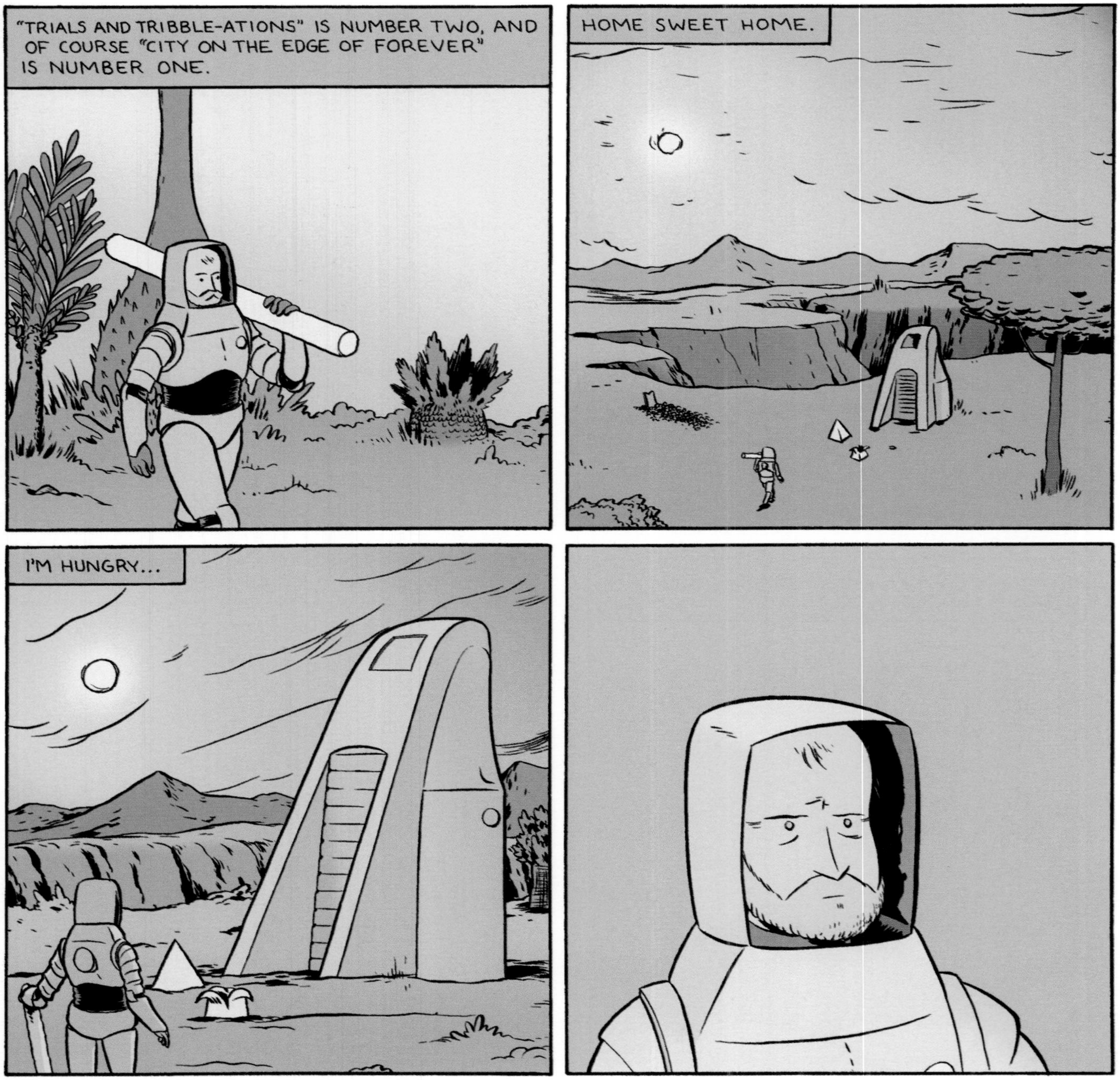
"TRIALS AND TRIBBLE-ATIONS" IS NUMBER TWO, AND OF COURSE "CITY ON THE EDGE OF FOREVER" IS NUMBER ONE.
HOME SWEET HOME.
I'M HUNGRY...

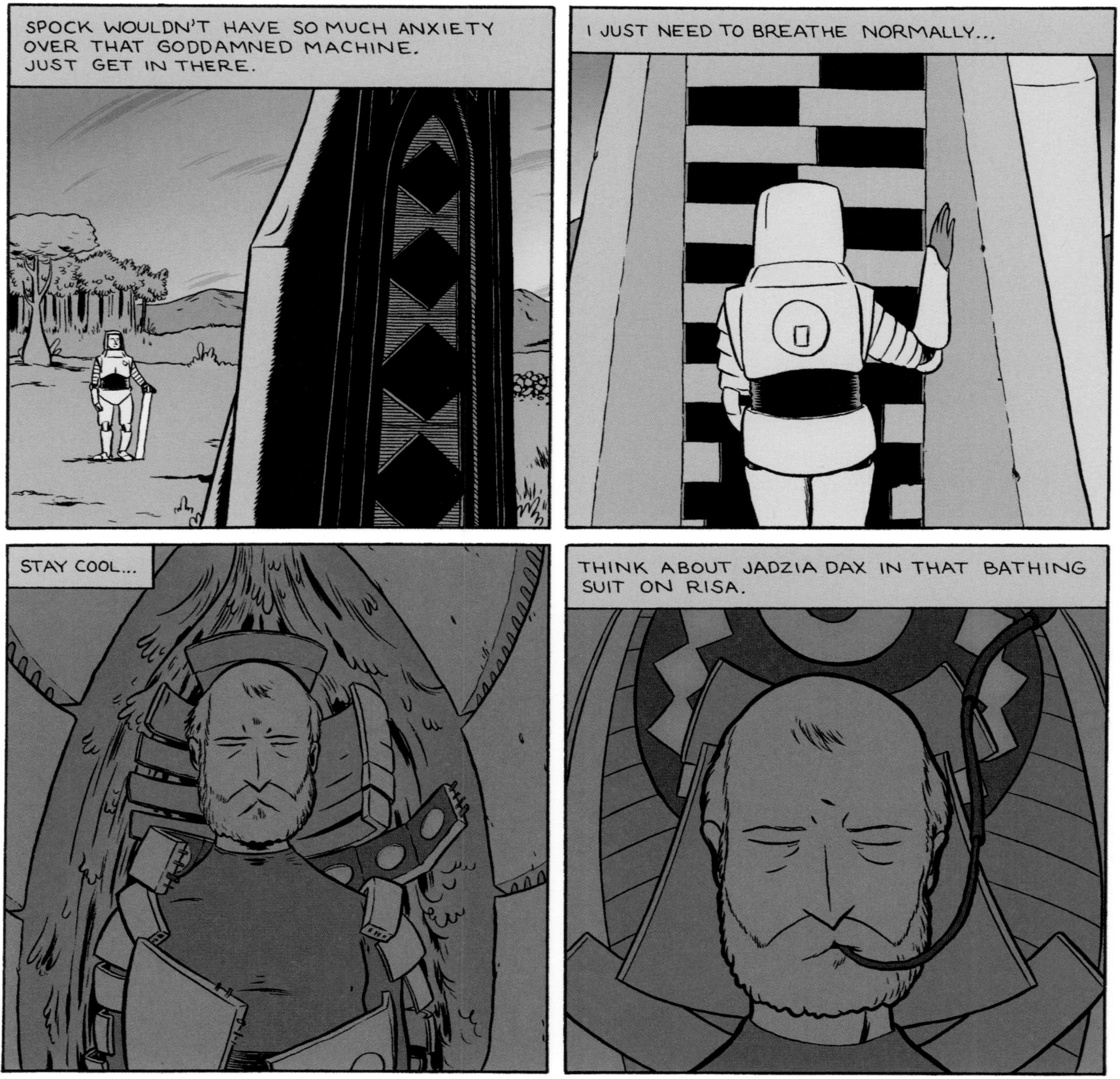
SPOCK WOULDN'T HAVE SO MUCH ANXIETY OVER THAT GODDAMNED MACHINE. JUST GET IN THERE.
I JUST NEED TO BREATHE NORMALLY...
STAY COOL...
THINK ABOUT JADZIA DAX IN THAT BATHING SUIT ON RISA.

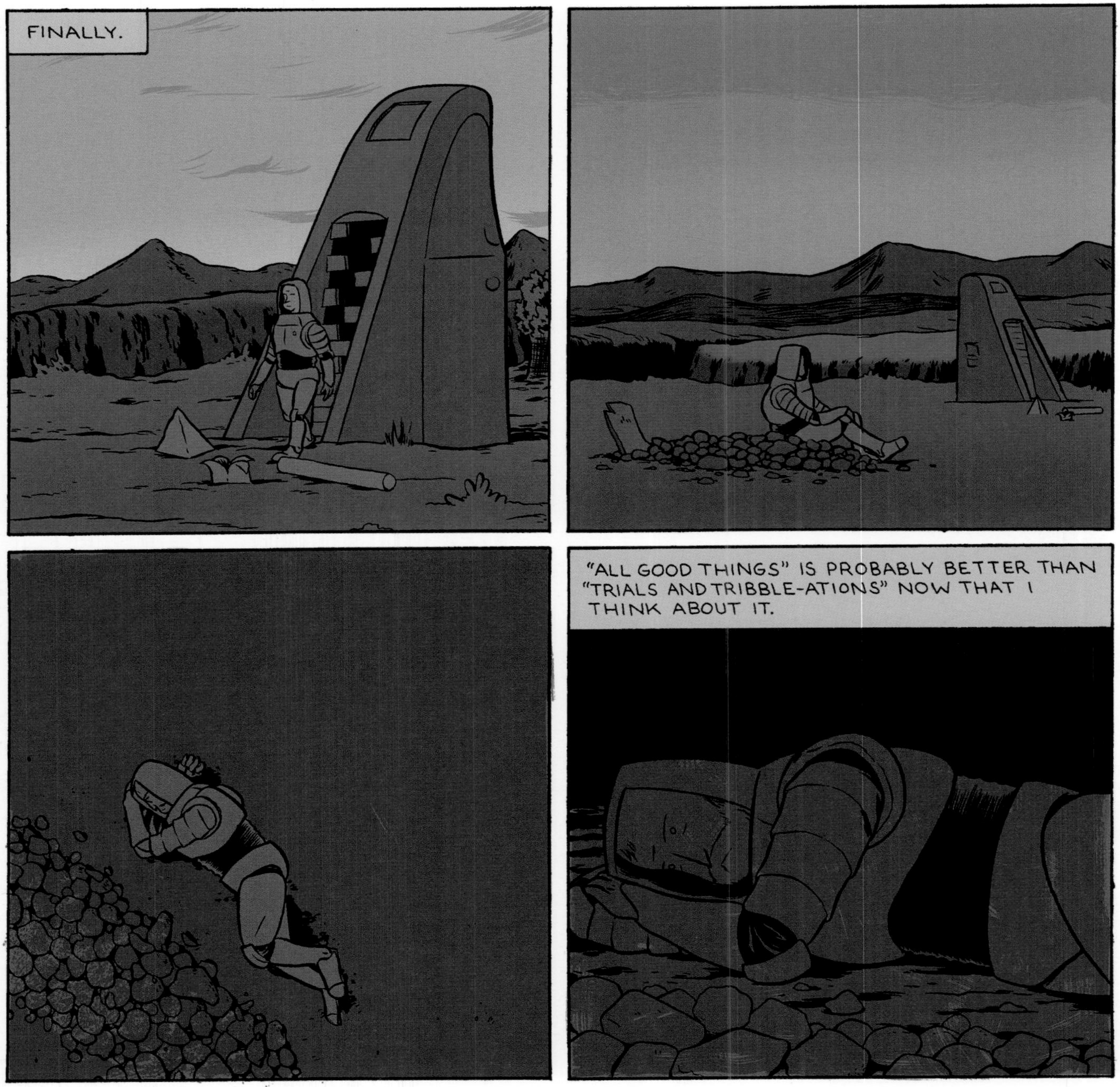
FINALLY.
"ALL GOOD THINGS" IS PROBABLY BETTER THAN "TRIALS AND TRIBBLE-ATIONS" NOW THAT I THINK ABOUT IT.

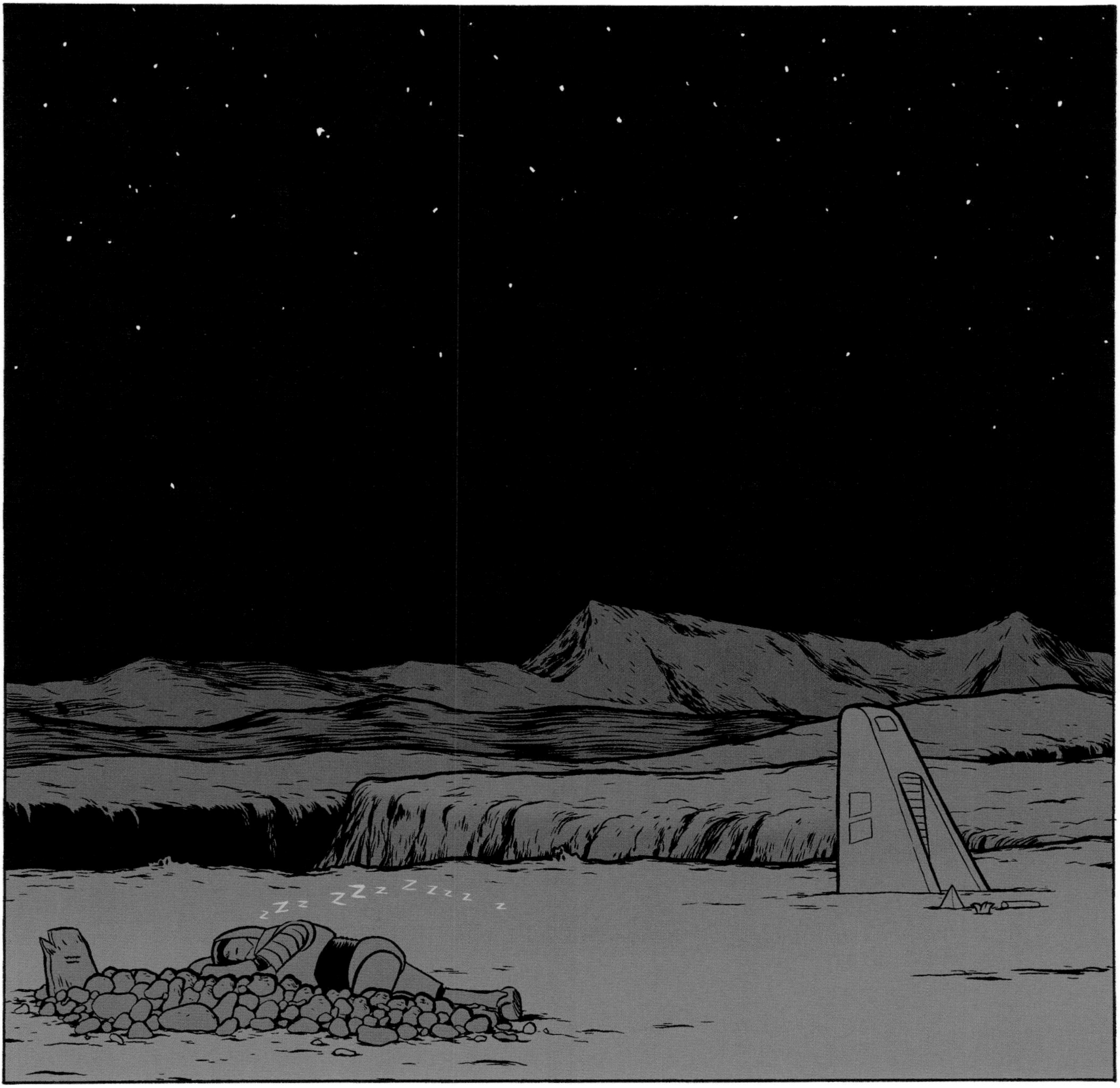

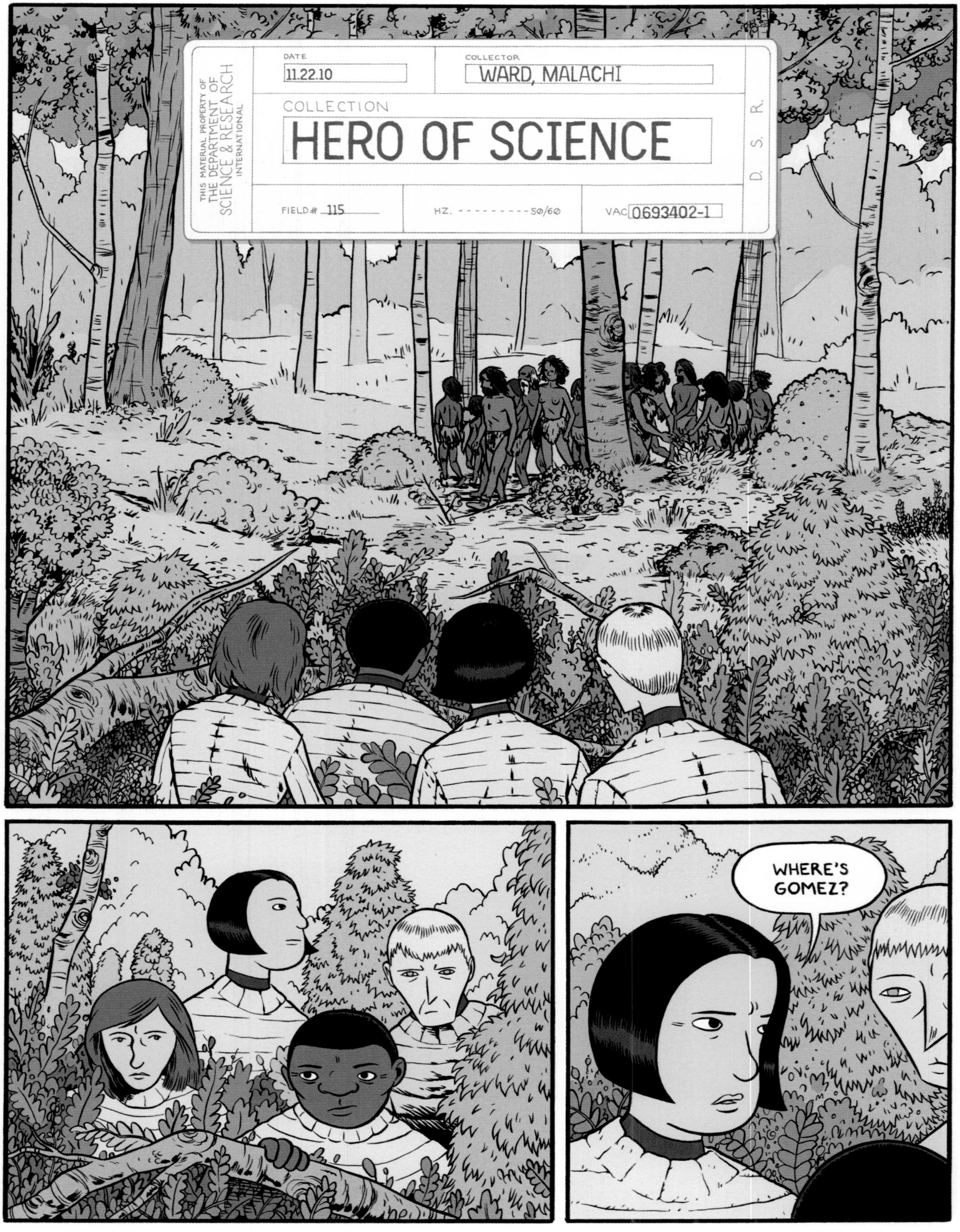
THIS MATERIAL PROPERTY OF THE DEPARTMENT OF SCIENCE & RESEARCH INTERNATIONAL
DATE 11.22.10
COLLECTOR WARD, MALACHI
COLLECTION
HERO OF SCIENCE
D. S. R.
FIELD# 115
HZ. ----------50/60
VAC 0693402-1
WHERE'S GOMEZ?

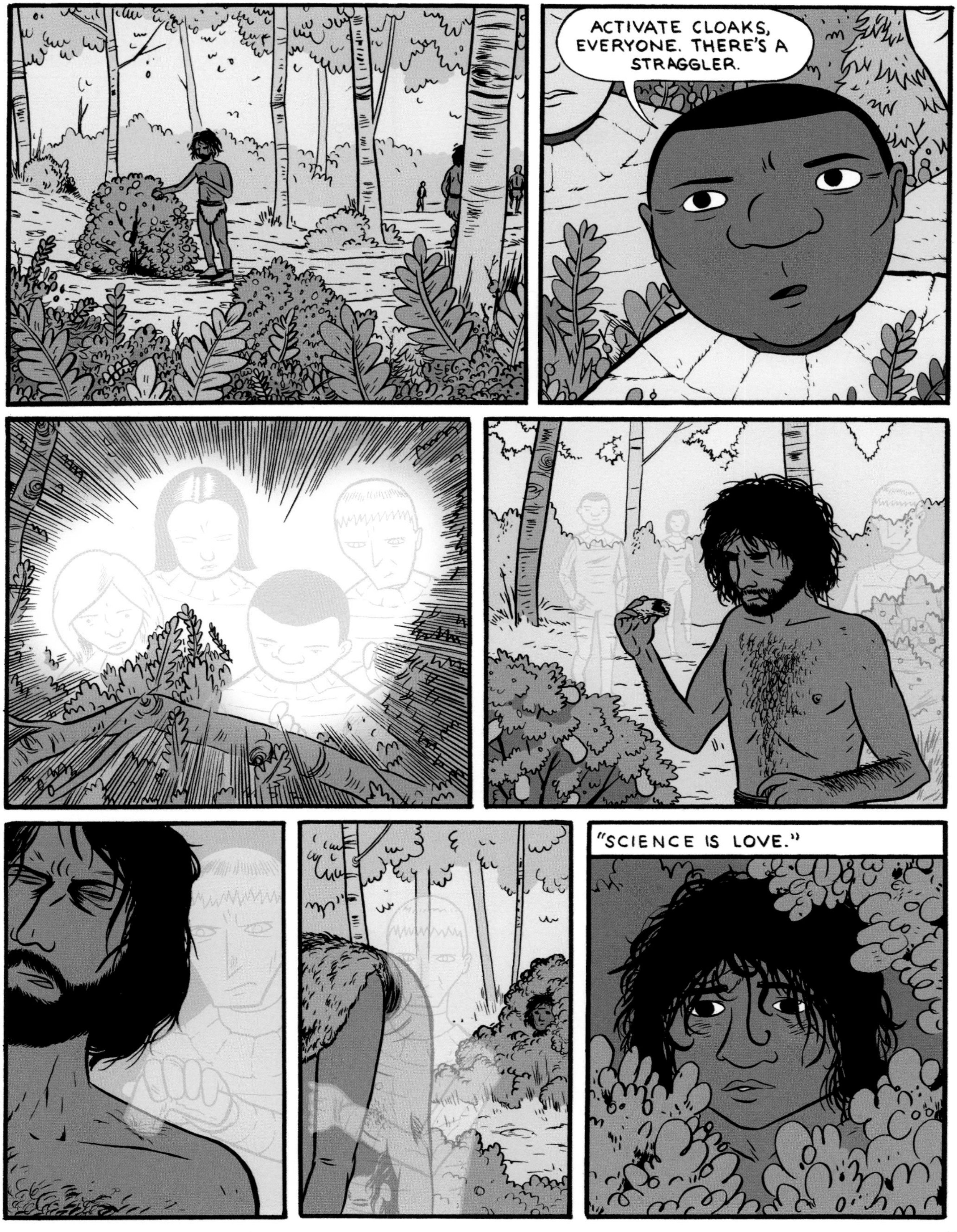
ACTIVATE CLOAKS, EVERYONE. THERE'S A STRAGGLER.
"SCIENCE IS LOVE."

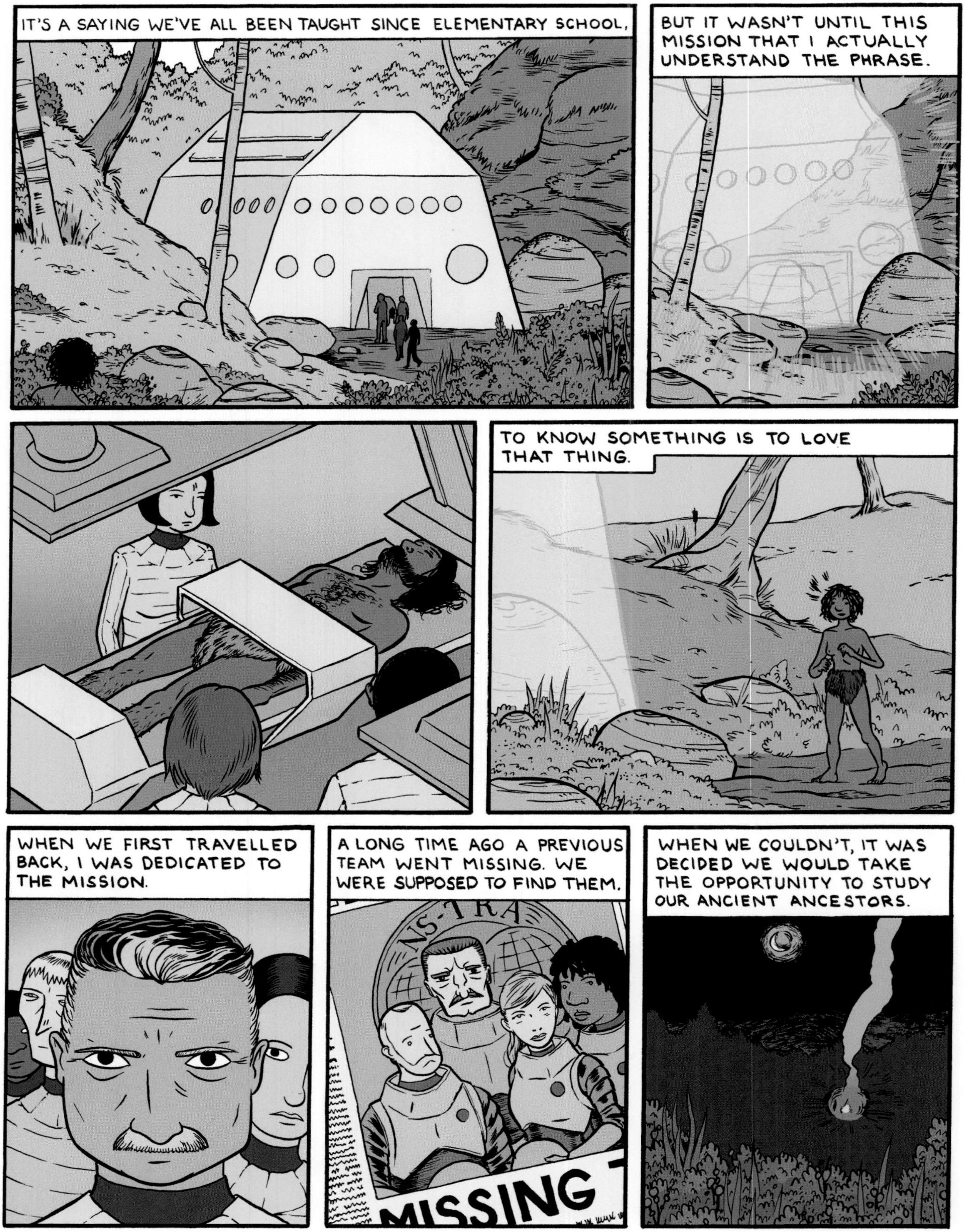
IT'S A SAYING WE'VE ALL BEEN TAUGHT SINCE ELEMENTARY SCHOOL,
BUT IT WASN'T UNTIL THIS MISSION THAT I ACTUALLY UNDERSTAND THE PHRASE.
TO KNOW SOMETHING IS TO LOVE THAT THING.
WHEN WE FIRST TRAVELLED BACK, I WAS DEDICATED TO THE MISSION.
A LONG TIME AGO A PREVIOUS TEAM WENT MISSING. WE WERE SUPPOSED TO FIND THEM.
MISSING
WHEN WE COULDN'T, IT WAS DECIDED WE WOULD TAKE THE OPPORTUNITY TO STUDY OUR ANCIENT ANCESTORS.

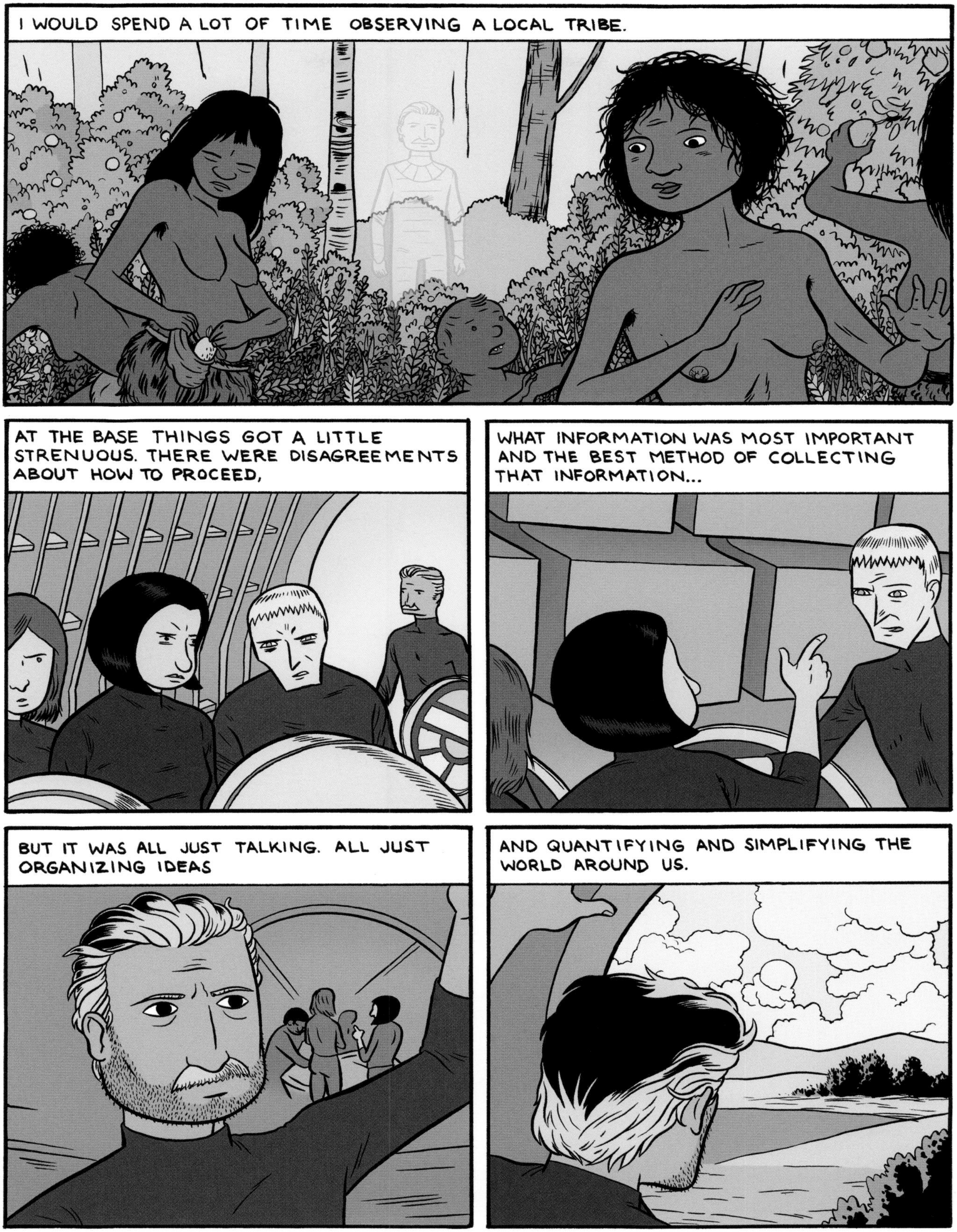
I WOULD SPEND A LOT OF TIME OBSERVING A LOCAL TRIBE.
AT THE BASE THINGS GOT A LITTLE STRENUOUS. THERE WERE DISAGREEMENTS ABOUT HOW TO PROCEED,
WHAT INFORMATION WAS MOST IMPORTANT AND THE BEST METHOD OF COLLECTING THAT INFORMATION...
BUT IT WAS ALL JUST TALKING. ALL JUST ORGANIZING IDEAS
AND QUANTIFYING AND SIMPLIFYING THE WORLD AROUND US.

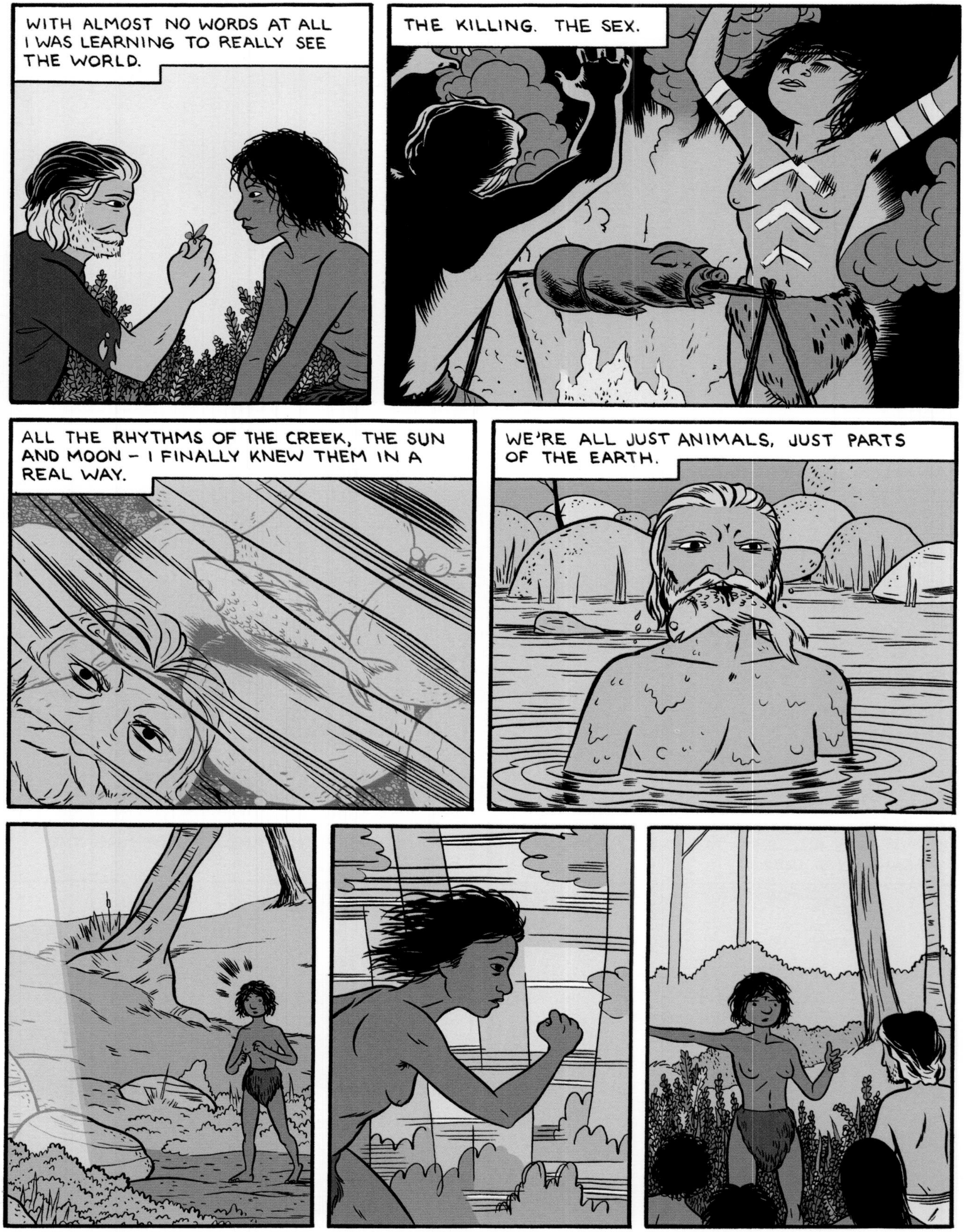
WITH ALMOST NO WORDS AT ALL I WAS LEARNING TO REALLY SEE THE WORLD.
THE KILLING. THE SEX.
ALL THE RHYTHMS OF THE CREEK, THE SUN AND MOON – I FINALLY KNEW THEM IN A REAL WAY.
WE'RE ALL JUST ANIMALS, JUST PARTS OF THE EARTH.

THEY DON'T KNOW THE WORLD, SO THEY DON'T KNOW ME.

THEY DON'T KNOW MY TRIBE.

FOR US, PROBLEMS HAVE SIMPLE, ELEGANT SOLUTIONS.

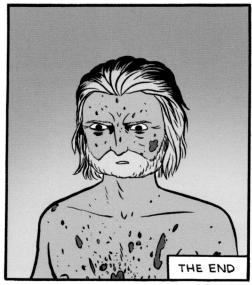

THE END

71

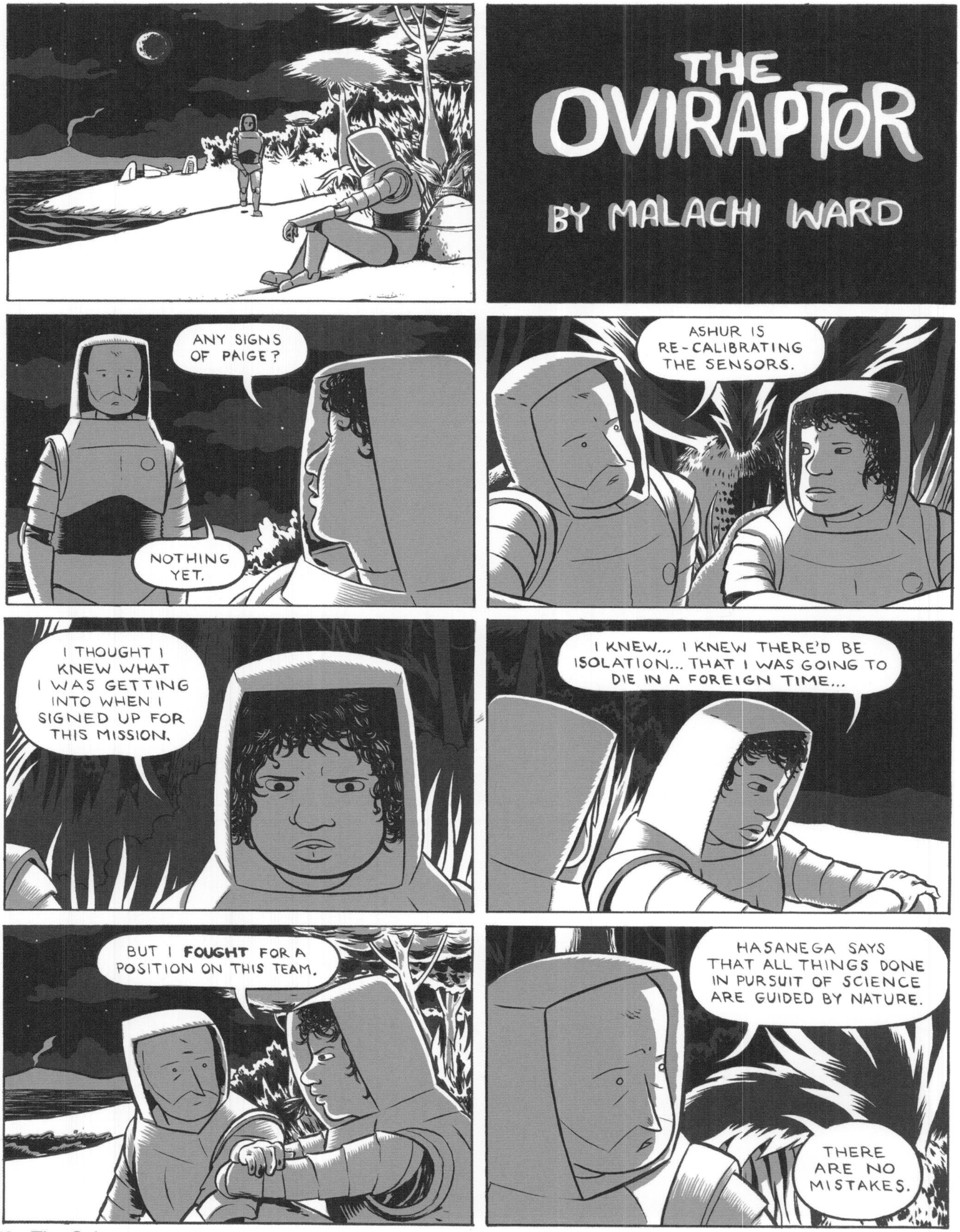
THE OVIRAPTOR
BY MALACHI WARD
ANY SIGNS OF PAIGE?
NOTHING YET.
ASHUR IS RE-CALIBRATING THE SENSORS.
I THOUGHT I KNEW WHAT I WAS GETTING INTO WHEN I SIGNED UP FOR THIS MISSION.
I KNEW... I KNEW THERE'D BE ISOLATION... THAT I WAS GOING TO DIE IN A FOREIGN TIME...
BUT I **FOUGHT** FOR A POSITION ON THIS TEAM.
HASANEGA SAYS THAT ALL THINGS DONE IN PURSUIT OF SCIENCE ARE GUIDED BY NATURE.
THERE ARE NO MISTAKES.

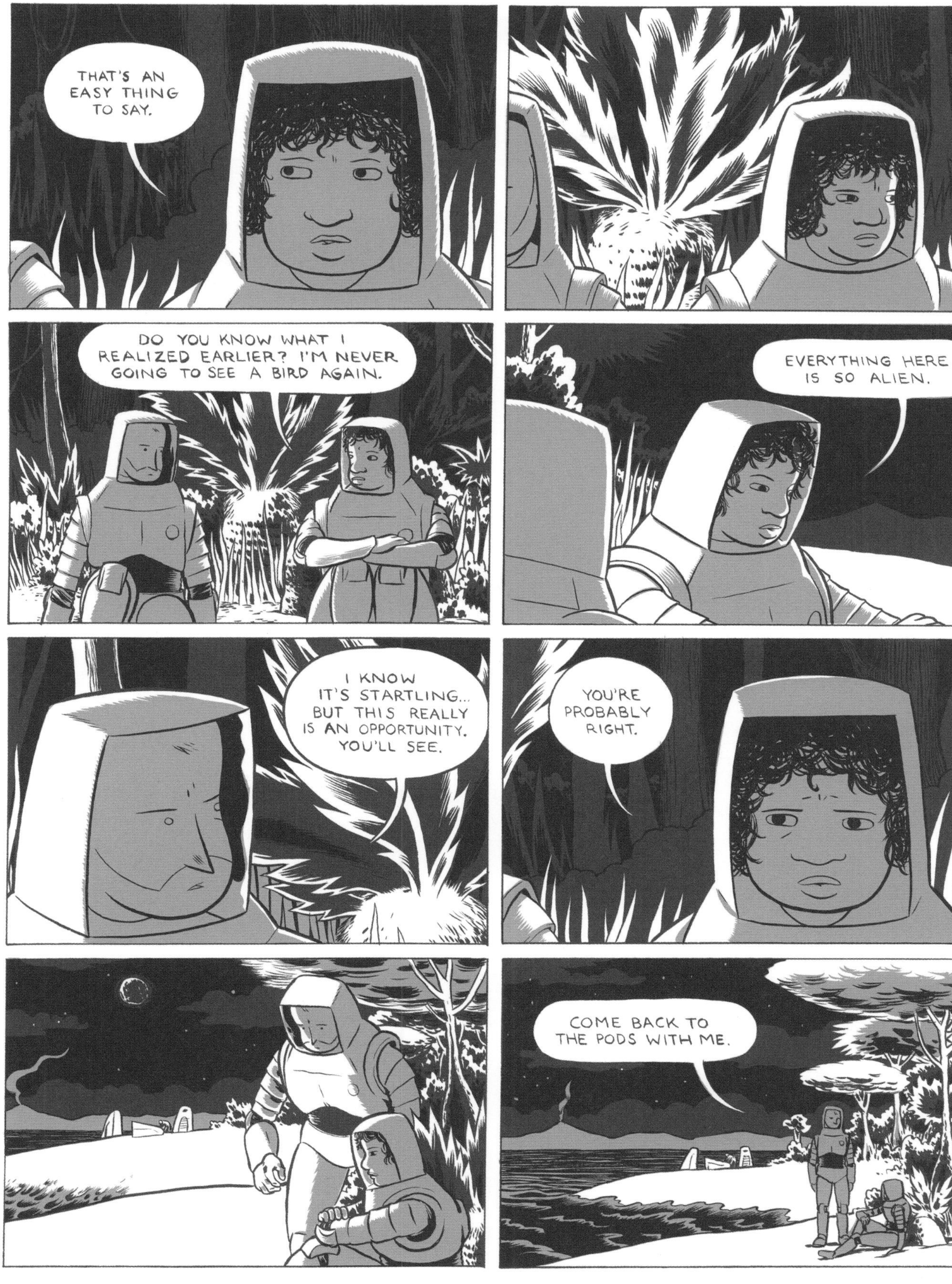
THAT'S AN EASY THING TO SAY.
DO YOU KNOW WHAT I REALIZED EARLIER? I'M NEVER GOING TO SEE A BIRD AGAIN.
EVERYTHING HERE IS SO ALIEN.
I KNOW IT'S STARTLING... BUT THIS REALLY IS AN OPPORTUNITY. YOU'LL SEE.
YOU'RE PROBABLY RIGHT.
COME BACK TO THE PODS WITH ME.

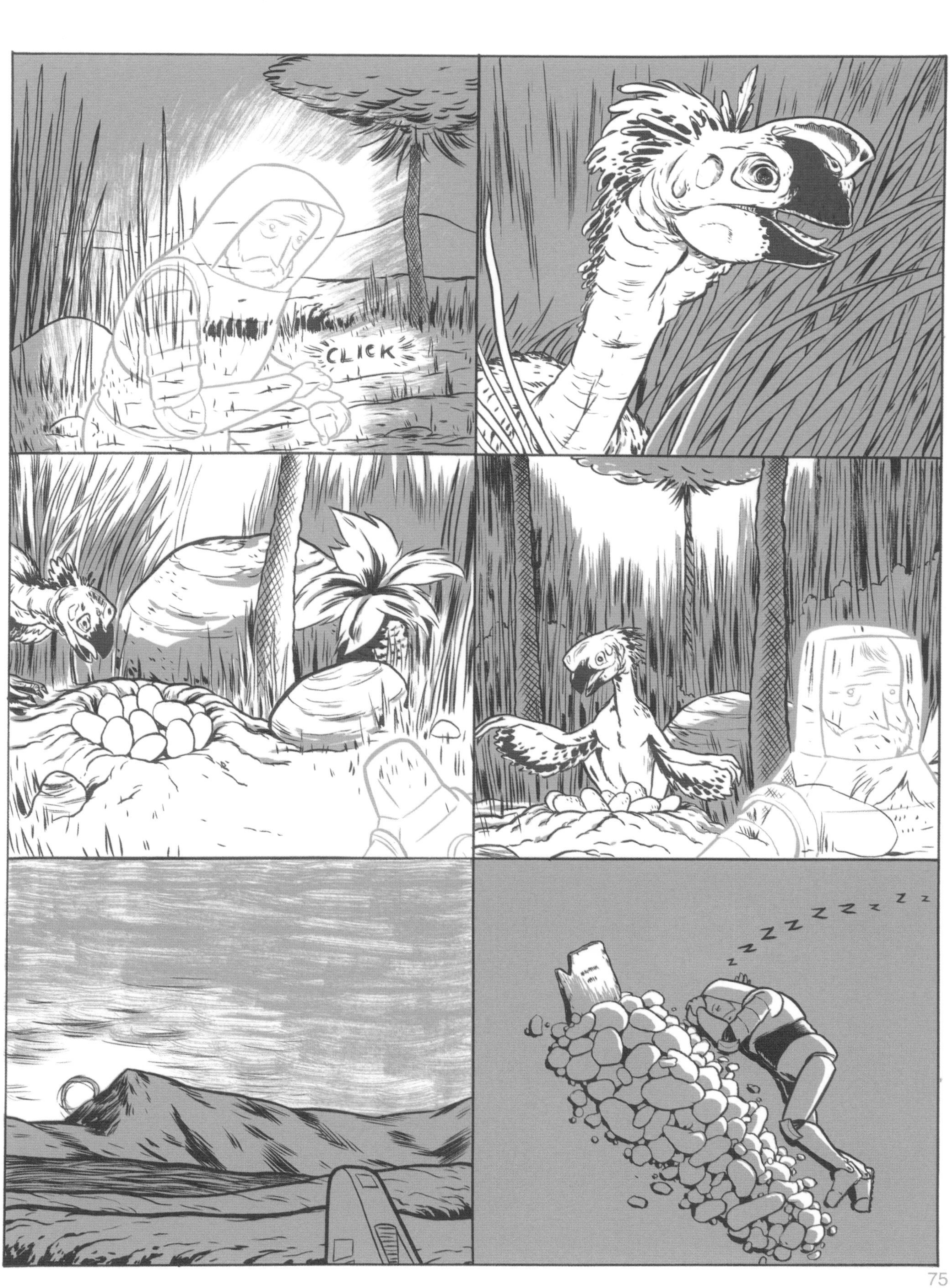
CLICK
z z Z Z Z Z Z z z Z z

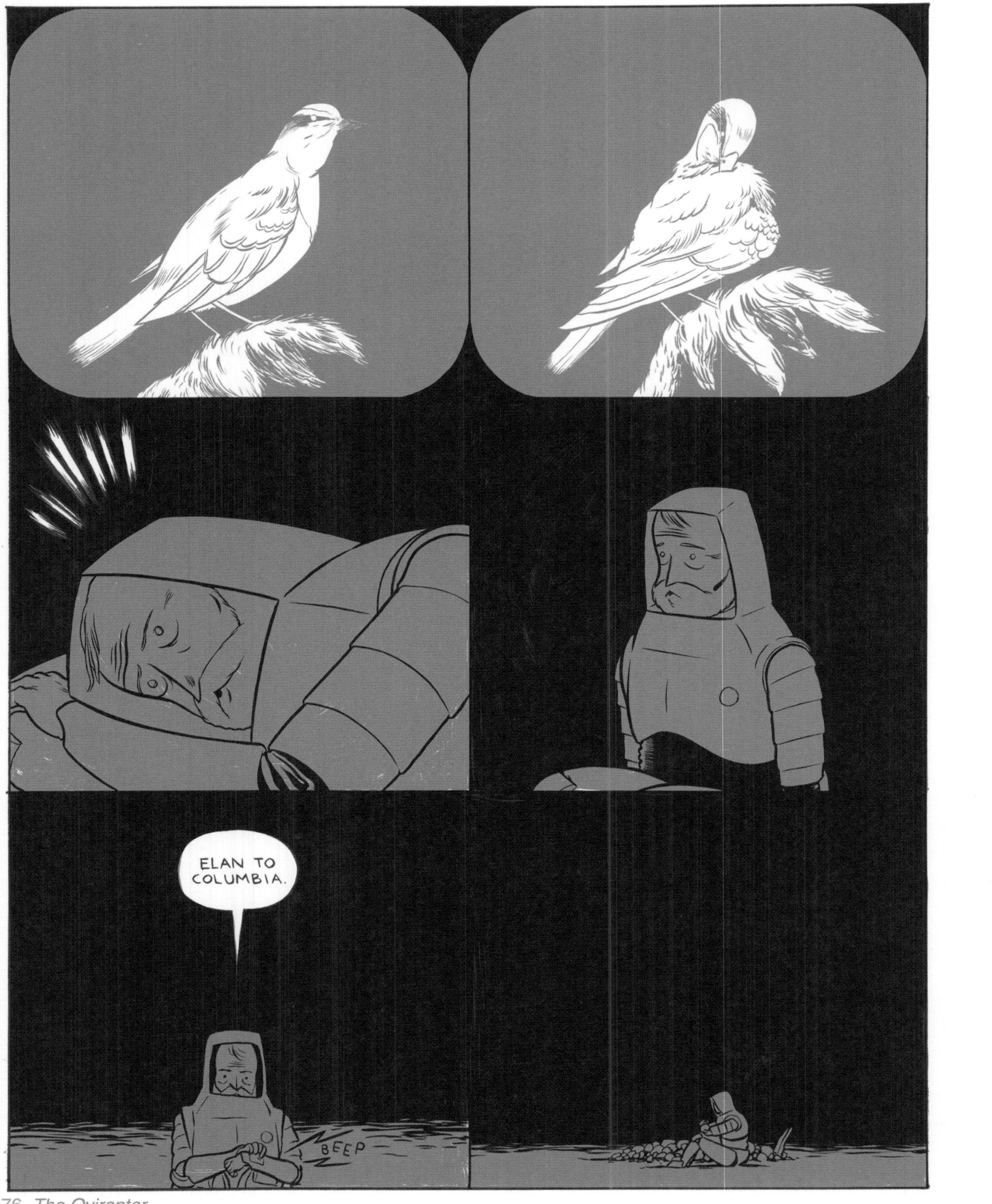
ELAN TO COLUMBIA.
BEEP

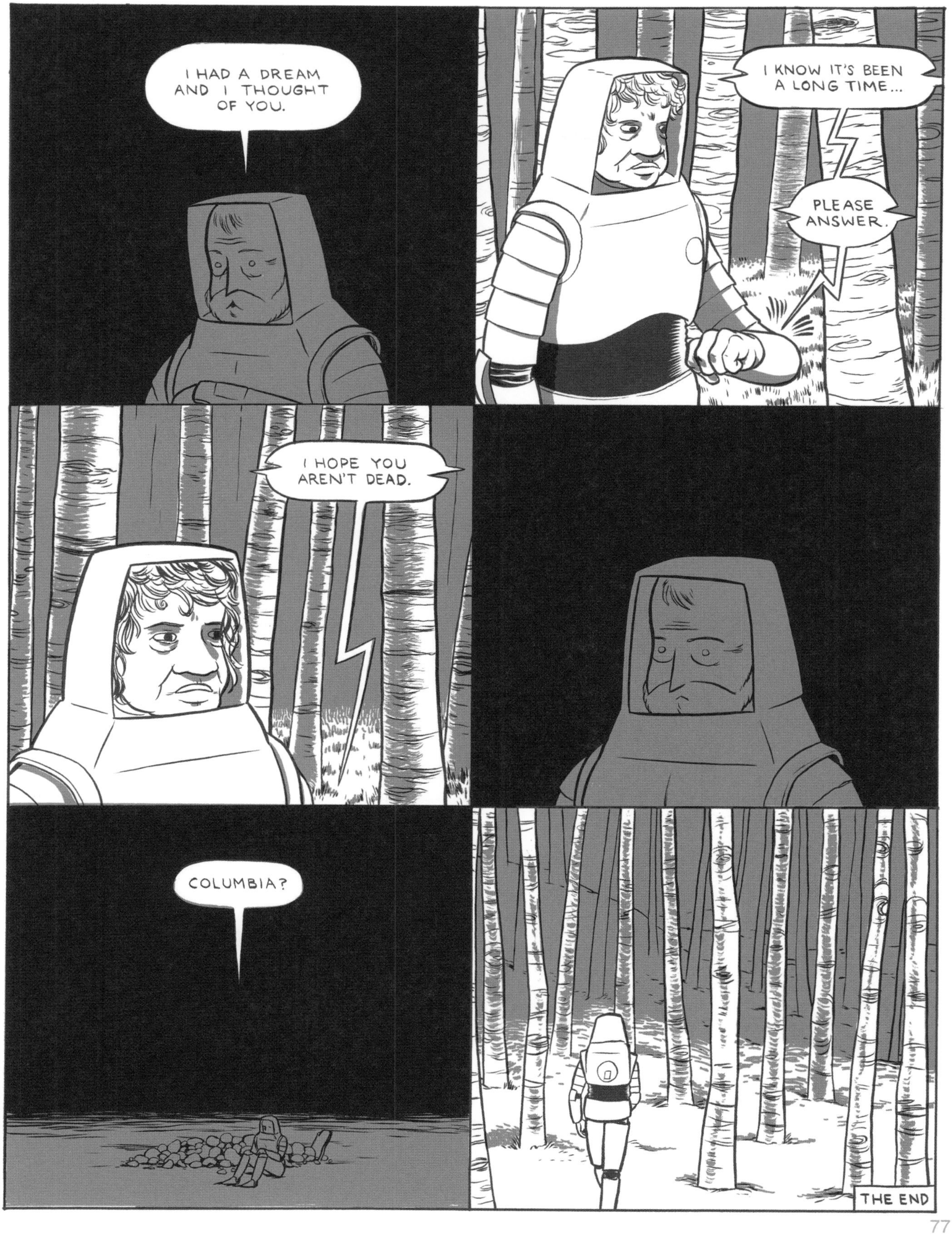
I HAD A DREAM AND I THOUGHT OF YOU.
I KNOW IT'S BEEN A LONG TIME...
PLEASE ANSWER.
I HOPE YOU AREN'T DEAD.
COLUMBIA?
THE END

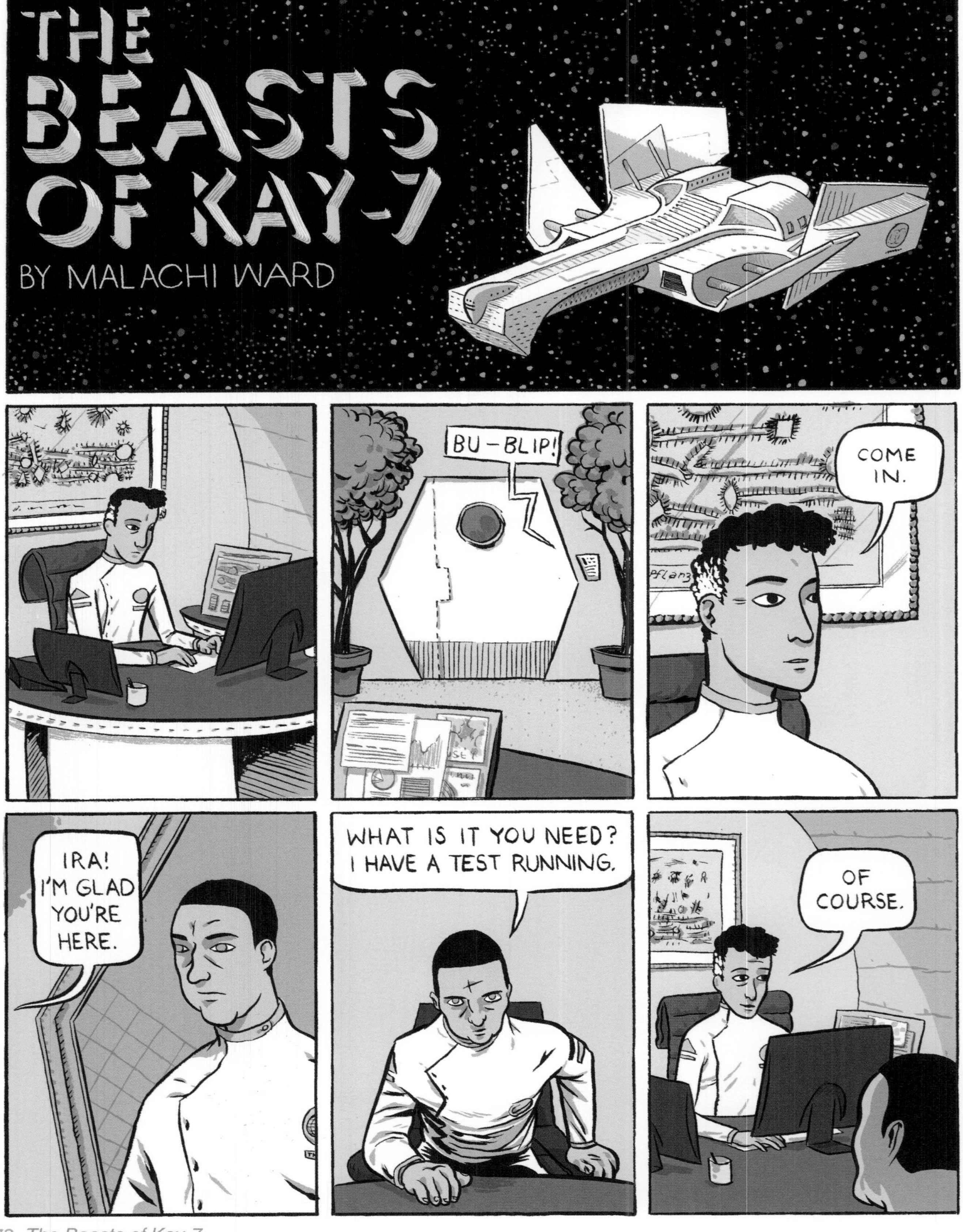
THE BEASTS OF KAY-7
BY MALACHI WARD
BU-BLIP!
COME IN.
IRA! I'M GLAD YOU'RE HERE.
WHAT IS IT YOU NEED? I HAVE A TEST RUNNING.
OF COURSE.

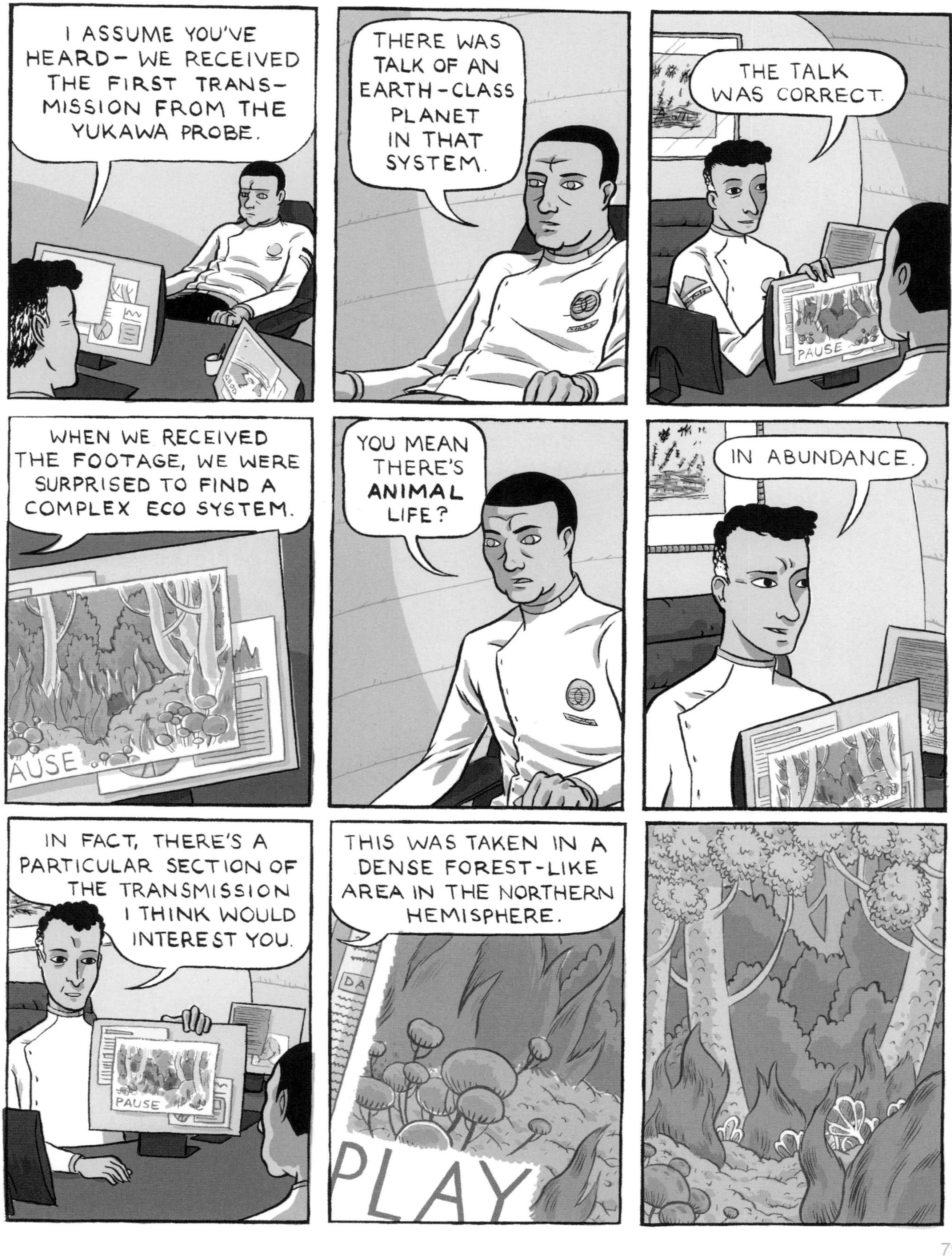
I ASSUME YOU'VE HEARD– WE RECEIVED THE FIRST TRANS-MISSION FROM THE YUKAWA PROBE.
THERE WAS TALK OF AN EARTH-CLASS PLANET IN THAT SYSTEM.
THE TALK WAS CORRECT.
PAUSE
WHEN WE RECEIVED THE FOOTAGE, WE WERE SURPRISED TO FIND A COMPLEX ECO SYSTEM.
AUSE
YOU MEAN THERE'S **ANIMAL** LIFE?
IN ABUNDANCE.
IN FACT, THERE'S A PARTICULAR SECTION OF THE TRANSMISSION I THINK WOULD INTEREST YOU.
PAUSE
THIS WAS TAKEN IN A DENSE FOREST-LIKE AREA IN THE NORTHERN HEMISPHERE.
PLAY

THE PROBE BARELY ESCAPED.

PLAY

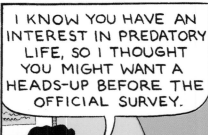
I KNOW YOU HAVE AN INTEREST IN PREDATORY LIFE, SO I THOUGHT YOU MIGHT WANT A HEADS-UP BEFORE THE OFFICIAL SURVEY.

WHEN IS THAT SCHEDULED?

A FEW MONTHS, I THINK.

IS IT POSSIBLE, SIR, FOR A SMALL TEAM TO LEAVE EARLIER?

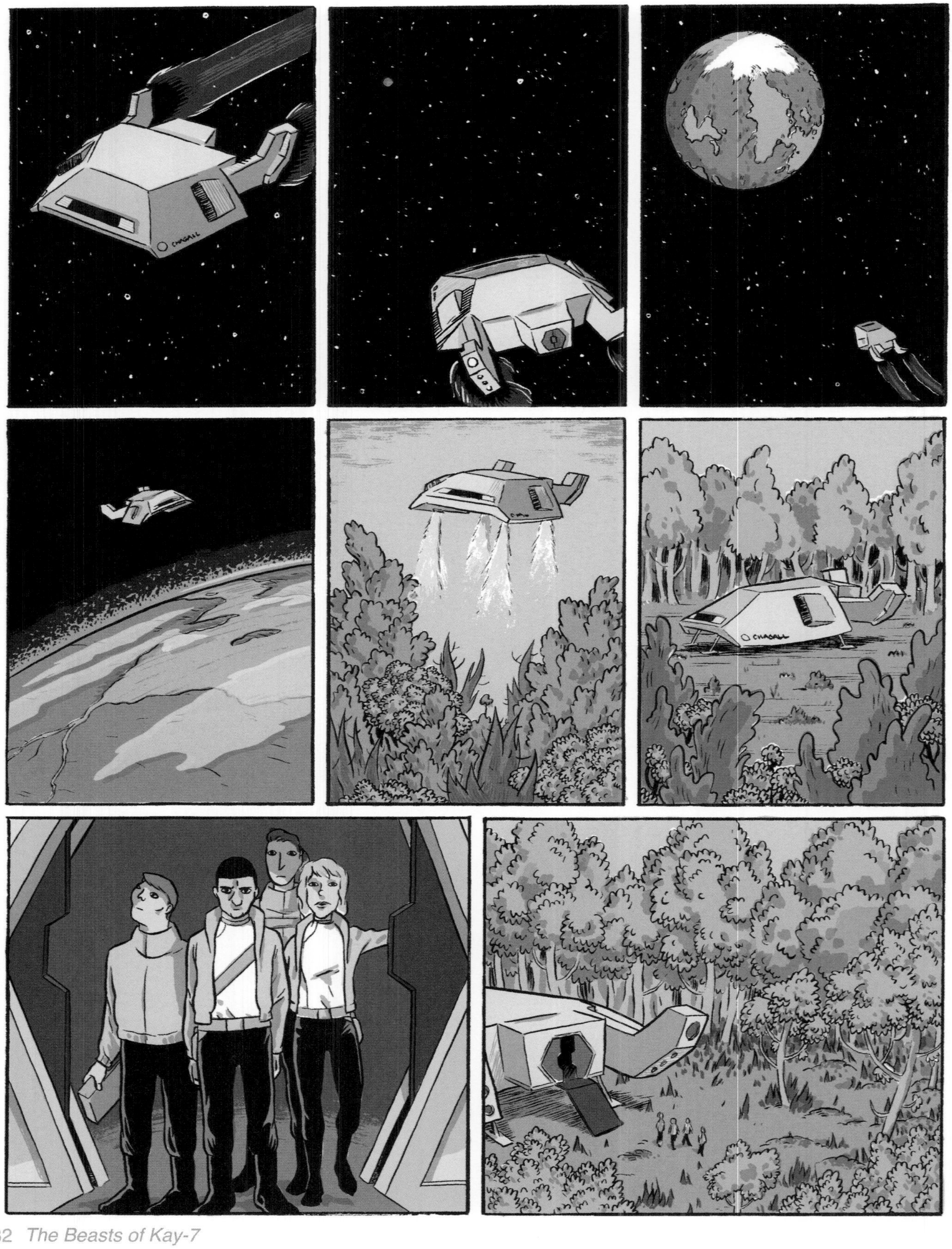
CHAGALL

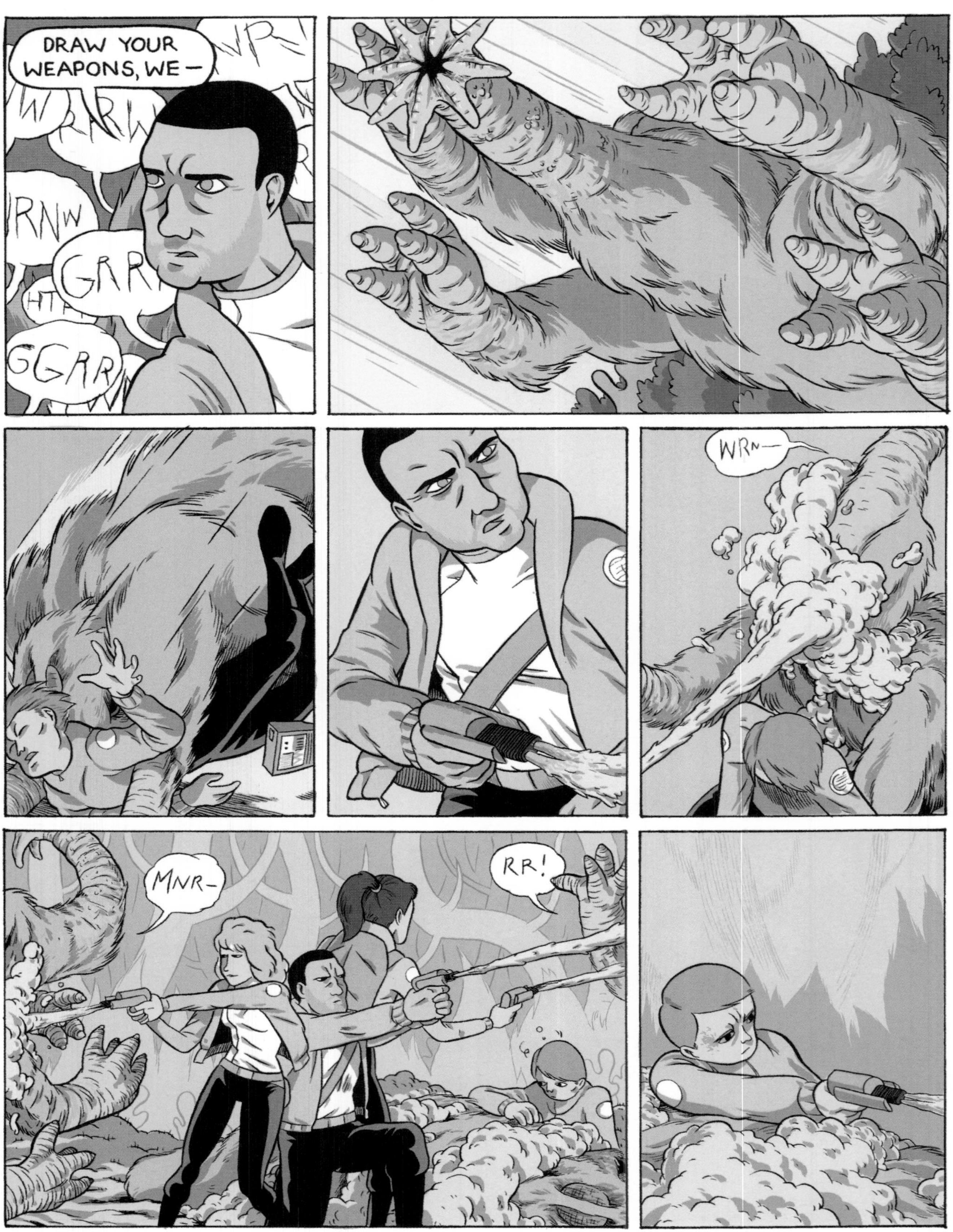
DRAW YOUR WEAPONS, WE—
WRN—
MNR-
RR!

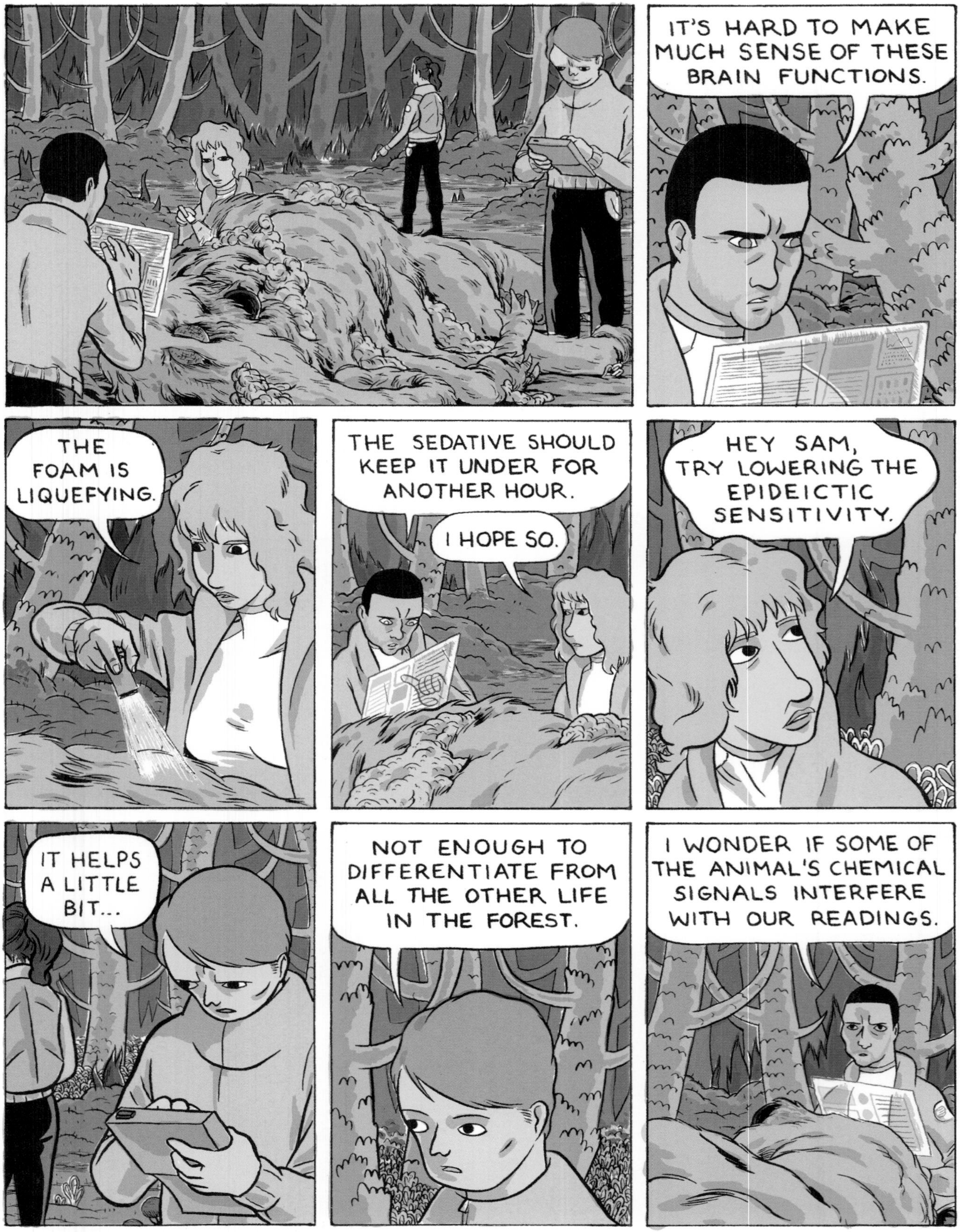
IT'S HARD TO MAKE MUCH SENSE OF THESE BRAIN FUNCTIONS.
THE FOAM IS LIQUEFYING.
THE SEDATIVE SHOULD KEEP IT UNDER FOR ANOTHER HOUR.
I HOPE SO.
HEY SAM, TRY LOWERING THE EPIDEICTIC SENSITIVITY.
IT HELPS A LITTLE BIT...
NOT ENOUGH TO DIFFERENTIATE FROM ALL THE OTHER LIFE IN THE FOREST.
I WONDER IF SOME OF THE ANIMAL'S CHEMICAL SIGNALS INTERFERE WITH OUR READINGS.

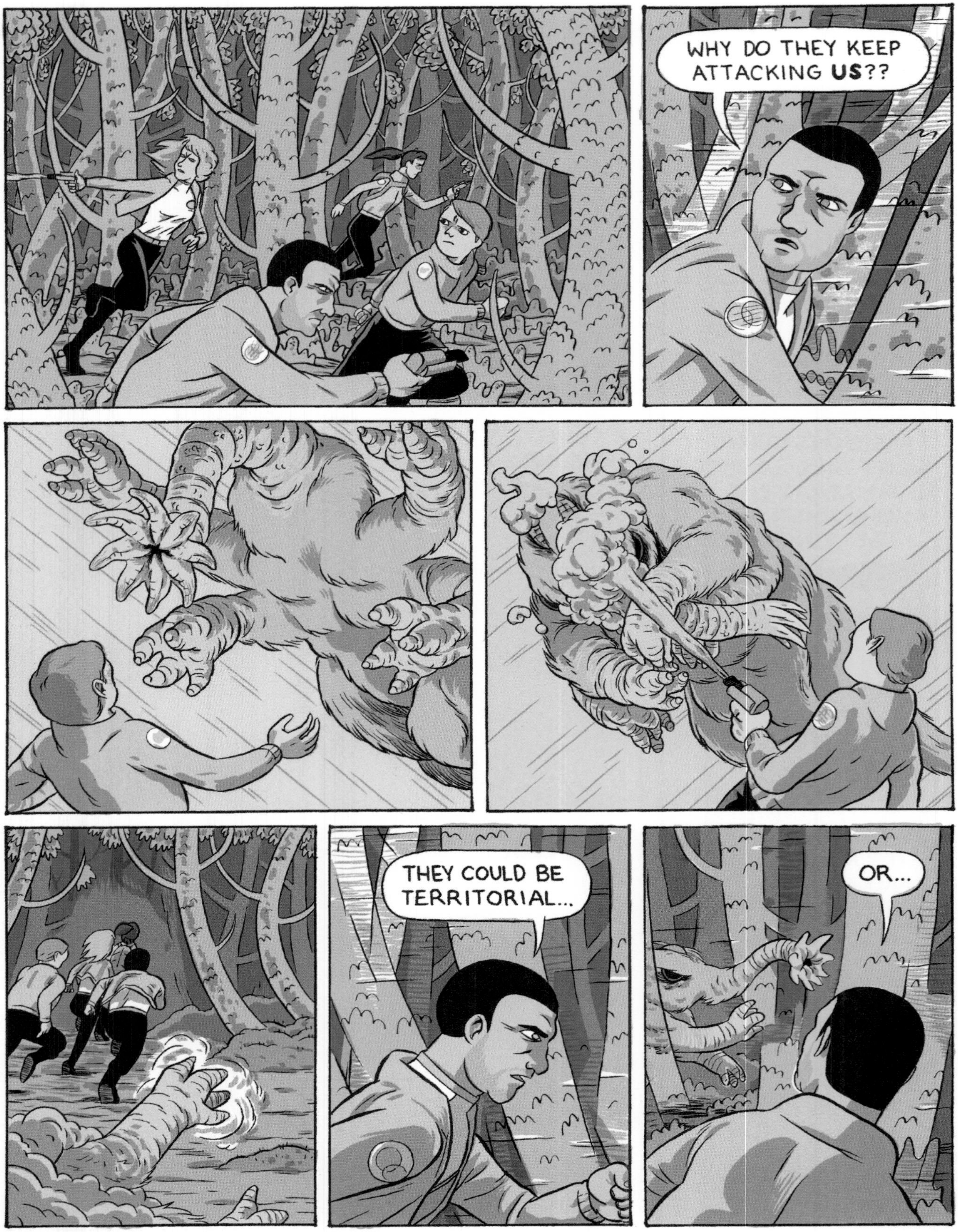
WHY DO THEY KEEP ATTACKING **US**??
THEY COULD BE TERRITORIAL...
OR...

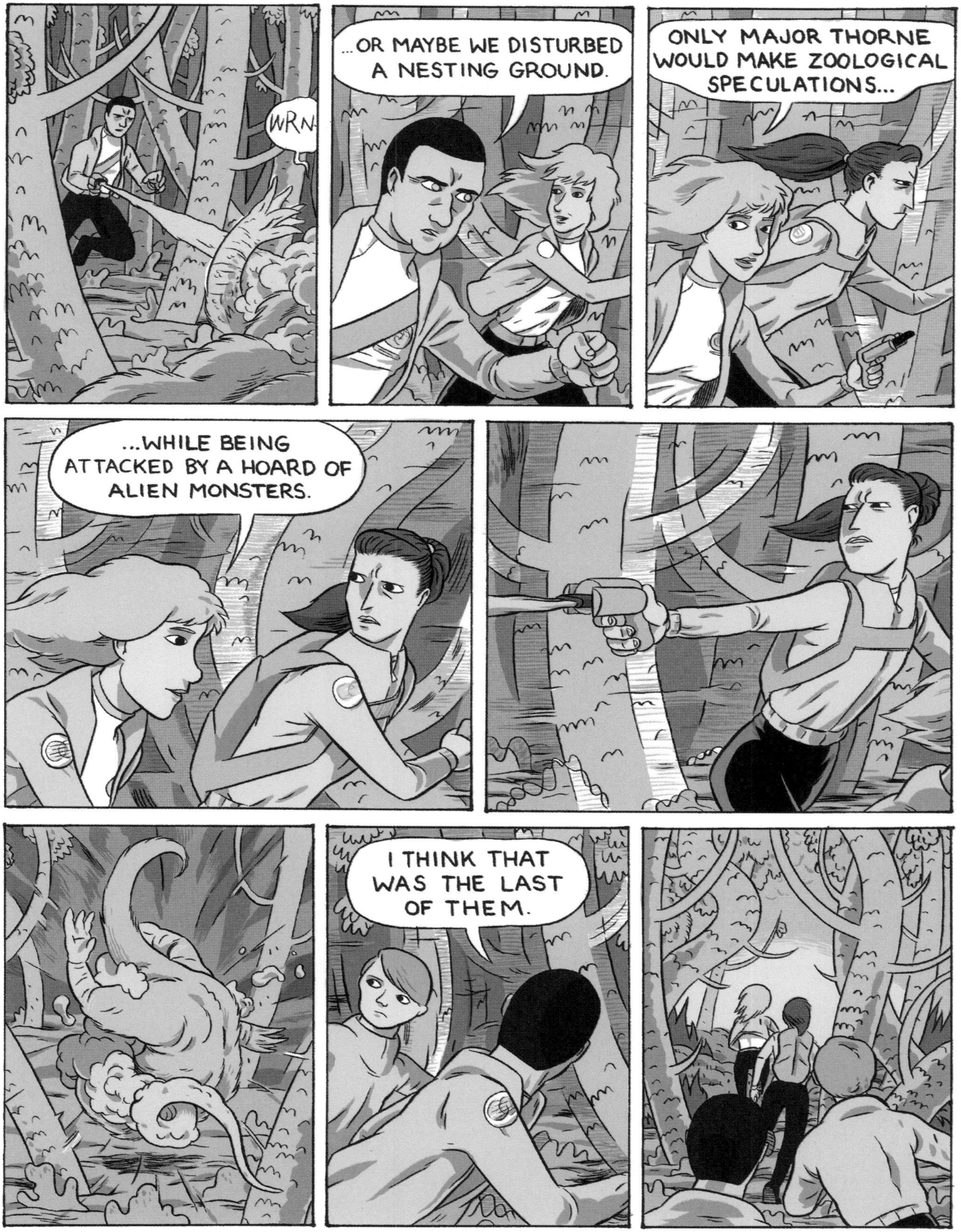
WRN
...OR MAYBE WE DISTURBED A NESTING GROUND.
ONLY MAJOR THORNE WOULD MAKE ZOOLOGICAL SPECULATIONS...
...WHILE BEING ATTACKED BY A HOARD OF ALIEN MONSTERS.
I THINK THAT WAS THE LAST OF THEM.

MORGAN, LOOK AT THIS.

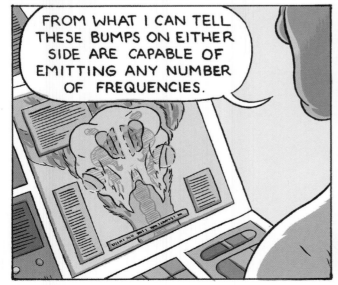

FROM WHAT I CAN TELL THESE BUMPS ON EITHER SIDE ARE CAPABLE OF EMITTING ANY NUMBER OF FREQUENCIES.

...SO IT COULD DEFLECT LEVEL THREE SCANS.

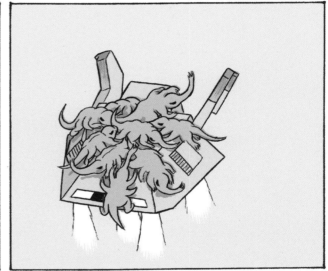

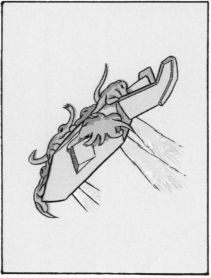

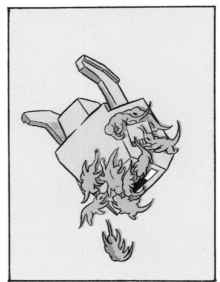

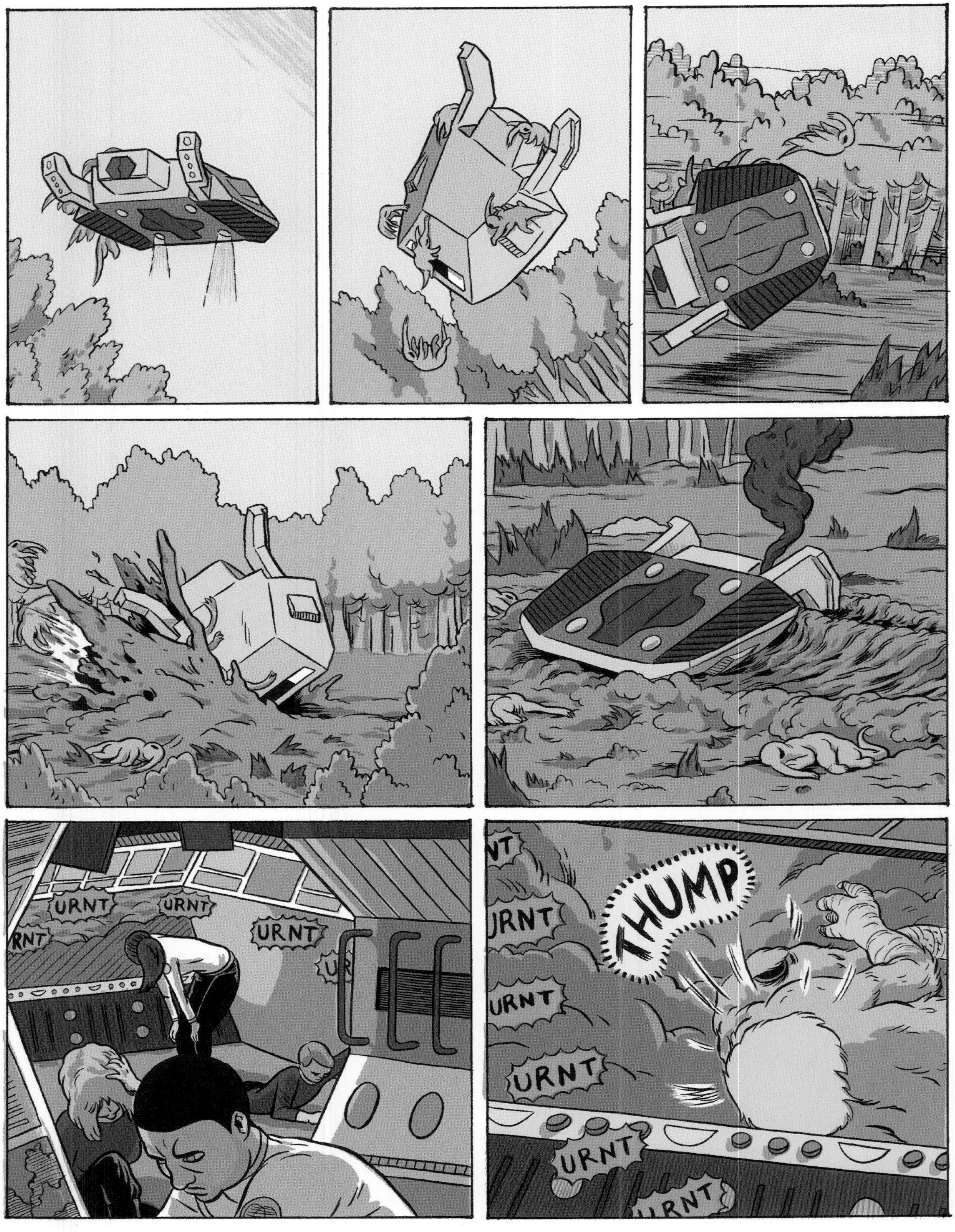
URNT
URNT
RNT
URNT
UR
NT
THUMP
RNT
URNT
URNT
URNT
URNT

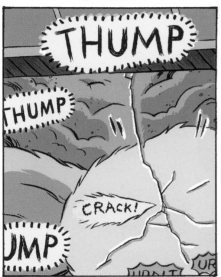

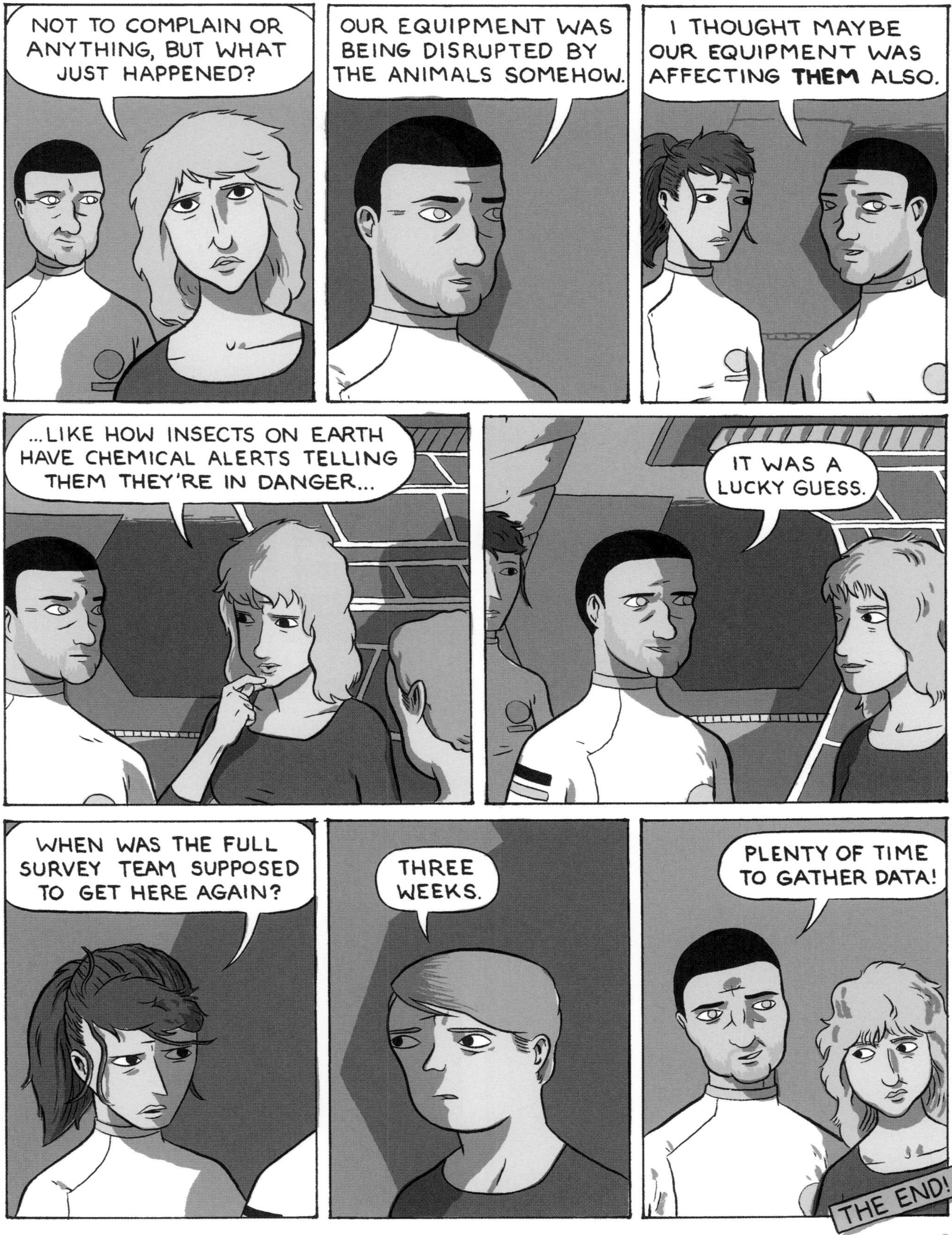
NOT TO COMPLAIN OR ANYTHING, BUT WHAT JUST HAPPENED?
OUR EQUIPMENT WAS BEING DISRUPTED BY THE ANIMALS SOMEHOW.
I THOUGHT MAYBE OUR EQUIPMENT WAS AFFECTING **THEM** ALSO.
...LIKE HOW INSECTS ON EARTH HAVE CHEMICAL ALERTS TELLING THEM THEY'RE IN DANGER...
IT WAS A LUCKY GUESS.
WHEN WAS THE FULL SURVEY TEAM SUPPOSED TO GET HERE AGAIN?
THREE WEEKS.
PLENTY OF TIME TO GATHER DATA!
THE END!

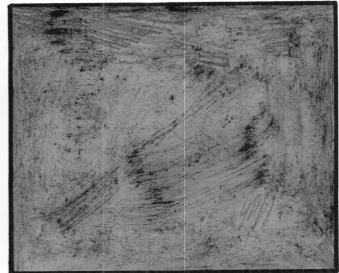

DISCONNECT

BY MALACHI WARD

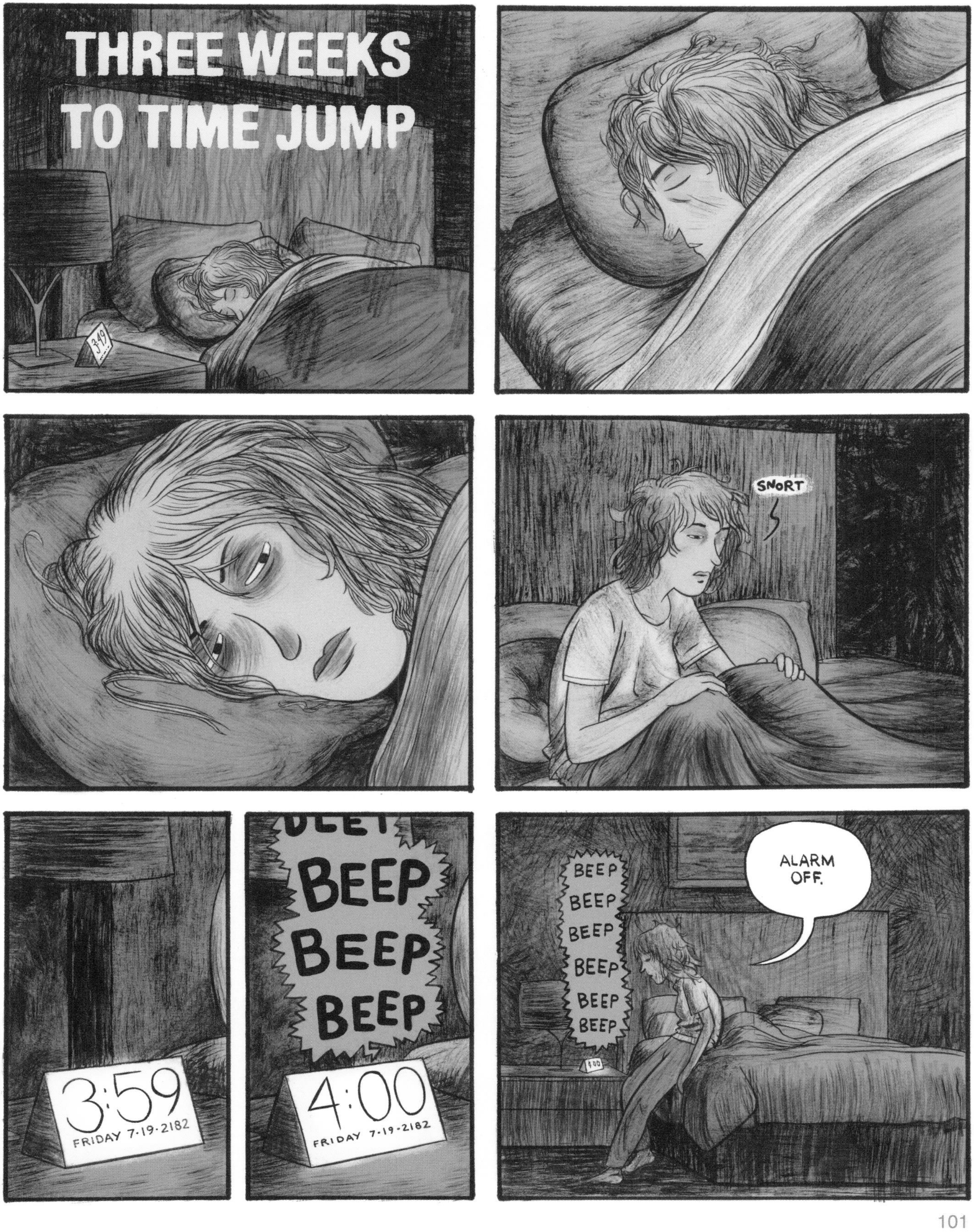
THREE WEEKS TO TIME JUMP
SNORT
3:59
FRIDAY 7·19·2182
BEEP
BEEP
BEEP
4:00
FRIDAY 7·19·2182
BEEP
BEEP
BEEP
BEEP
BEEP
BEEP
ALARM OFF.

* From "Analysis of one million base pairs of Neanderthal DNA" for NATURE. By Richard E. Green, Johannes Krause, Susan E. Ptak, Adrian W. Briggs, Michael T. Ronan, Jan F. Simons, Lei Du, Michael Egholm, Jonathan M. Rothberg, Maja Paunovic, and Svante Pääbo.

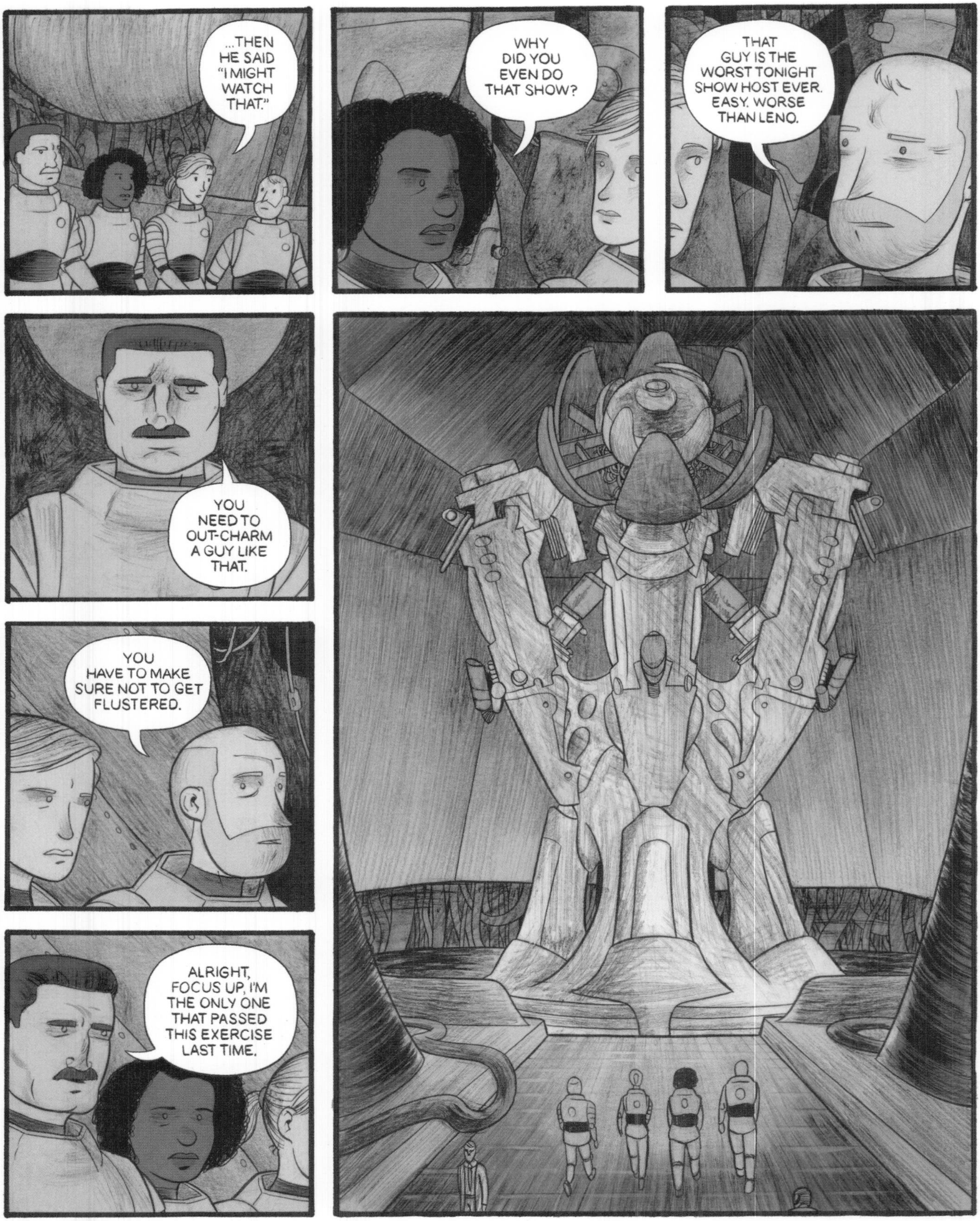
...THEN HE SAID "I MIGHT WATCH THAT."
WHY DID YOU EVEN DO THAT SHOW?
THAT GUY IS THE WORST TONIGHT SHOW HOST EVER. EASY. WORSE THAN LENO.
YOU NEED TO OUT-CHARM A GUY LIKE THAT.
YOU HAVE TO MAKE SURE NOT TO GET FLUSTERED.
ALRIGHT, FOCUS UP, I'M THE ONLY ONE THAT PASSED THIS EXERCISE LAST TIME.

SIX HOURS
TO TIME JUMP

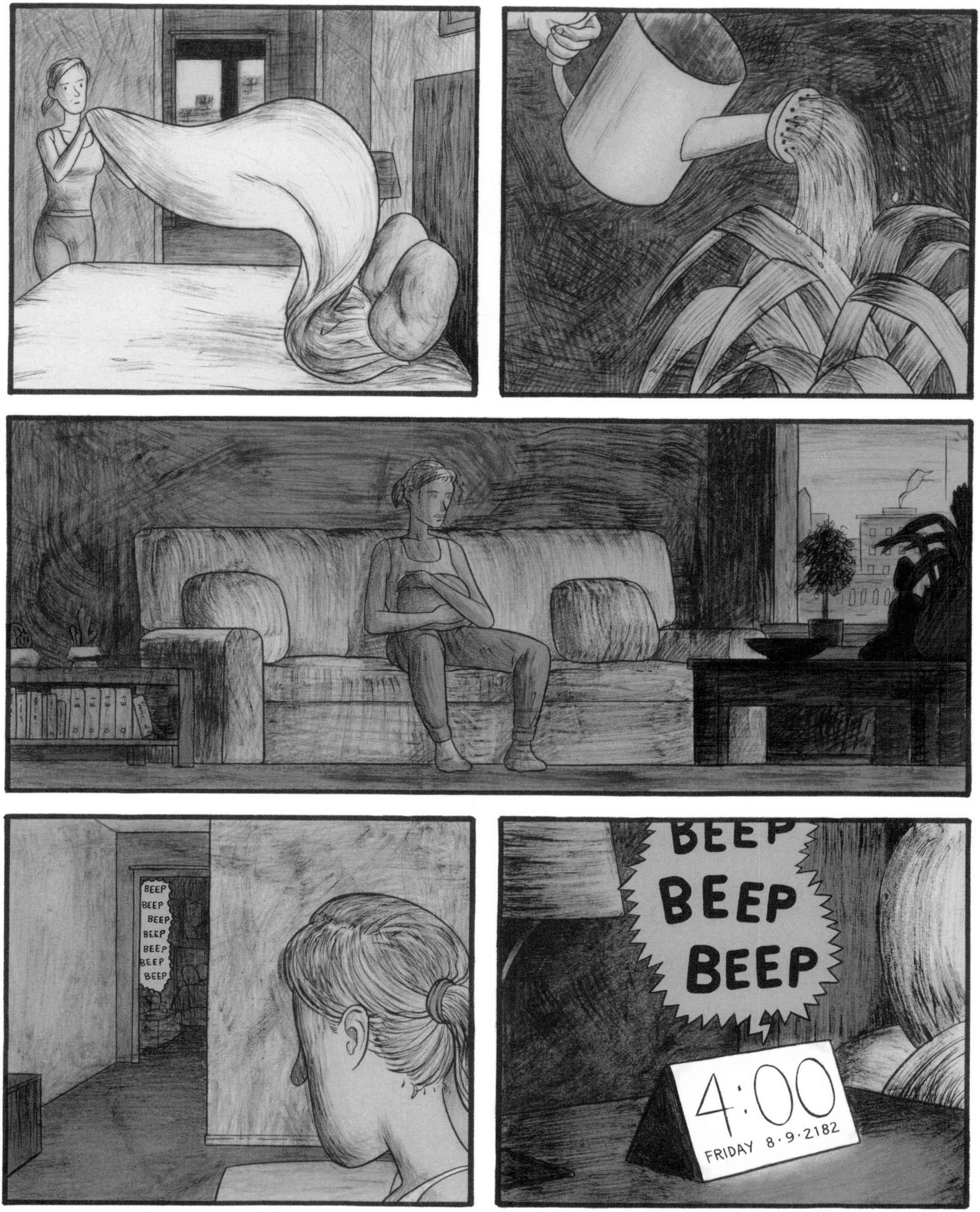
BEEP
BEEP
BEEP
BEEP
BEEP
BEEP
BEEP
BEEP
BEEP
4:00
FRIDAY 8·9·2182

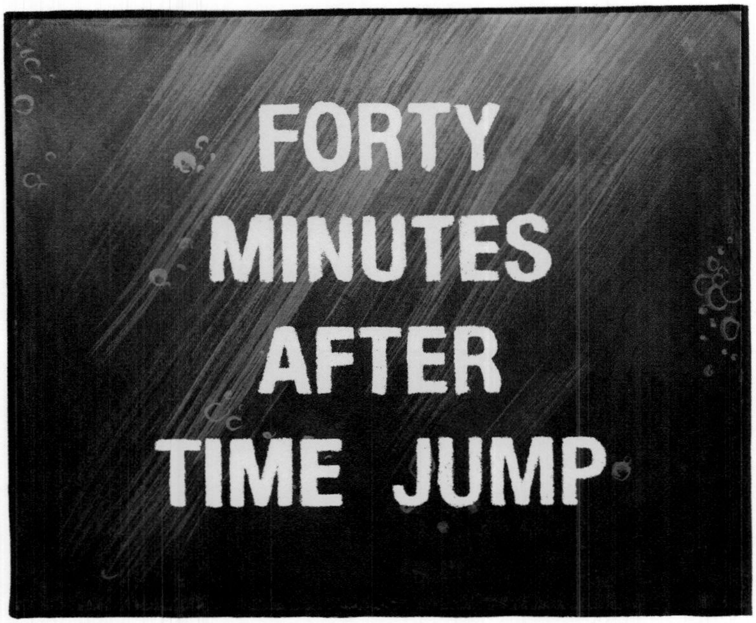
FORTY MINUTES AFTER TIME JUMP

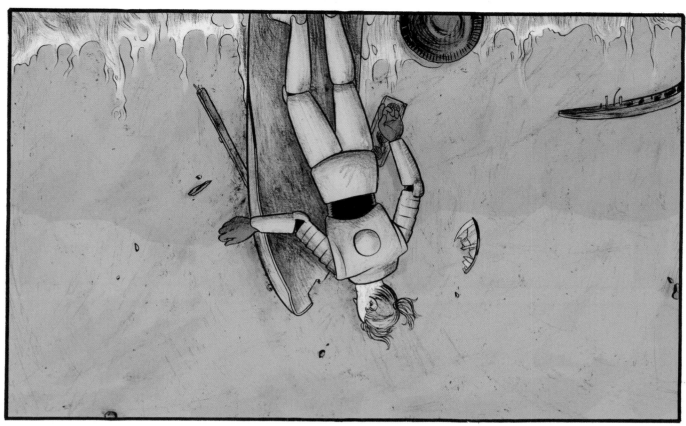

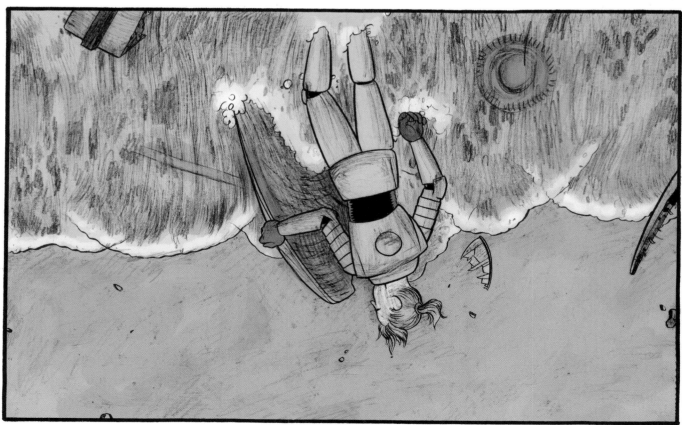

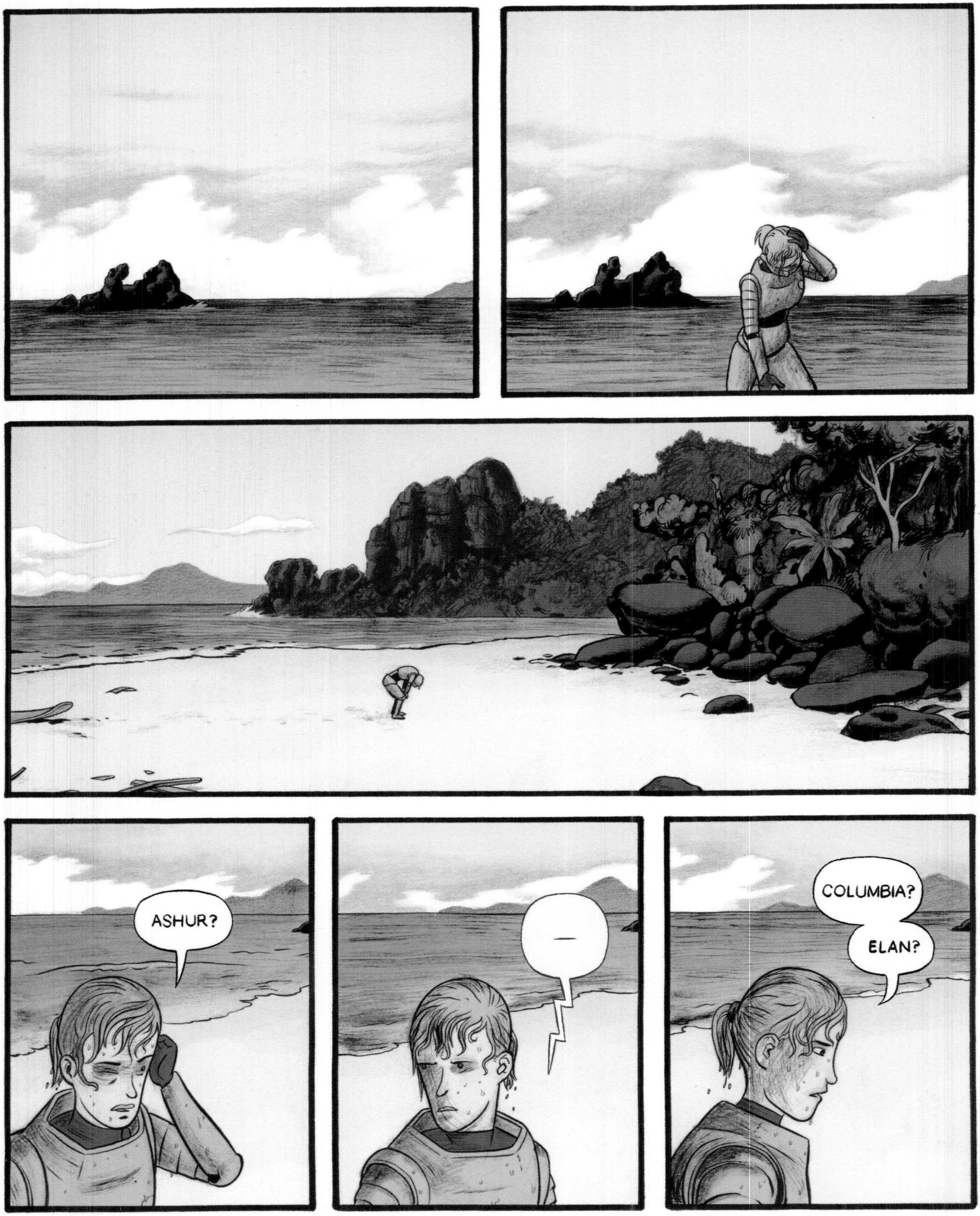
ASHUR?
—
COLUMBIA?
ELAN?

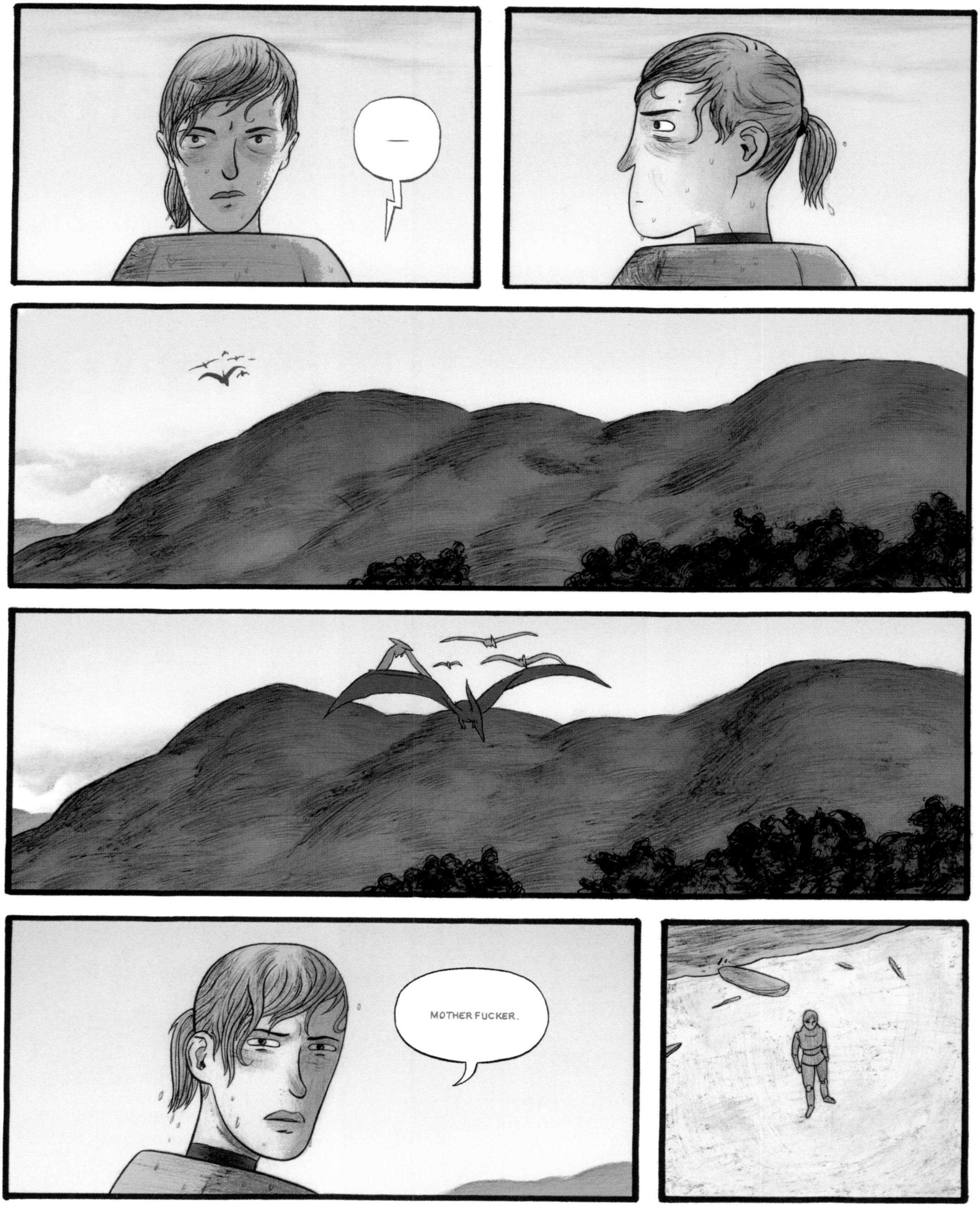
—
MOTHER FUCKER.

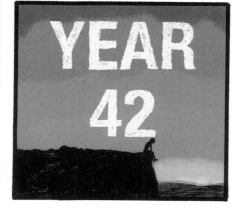

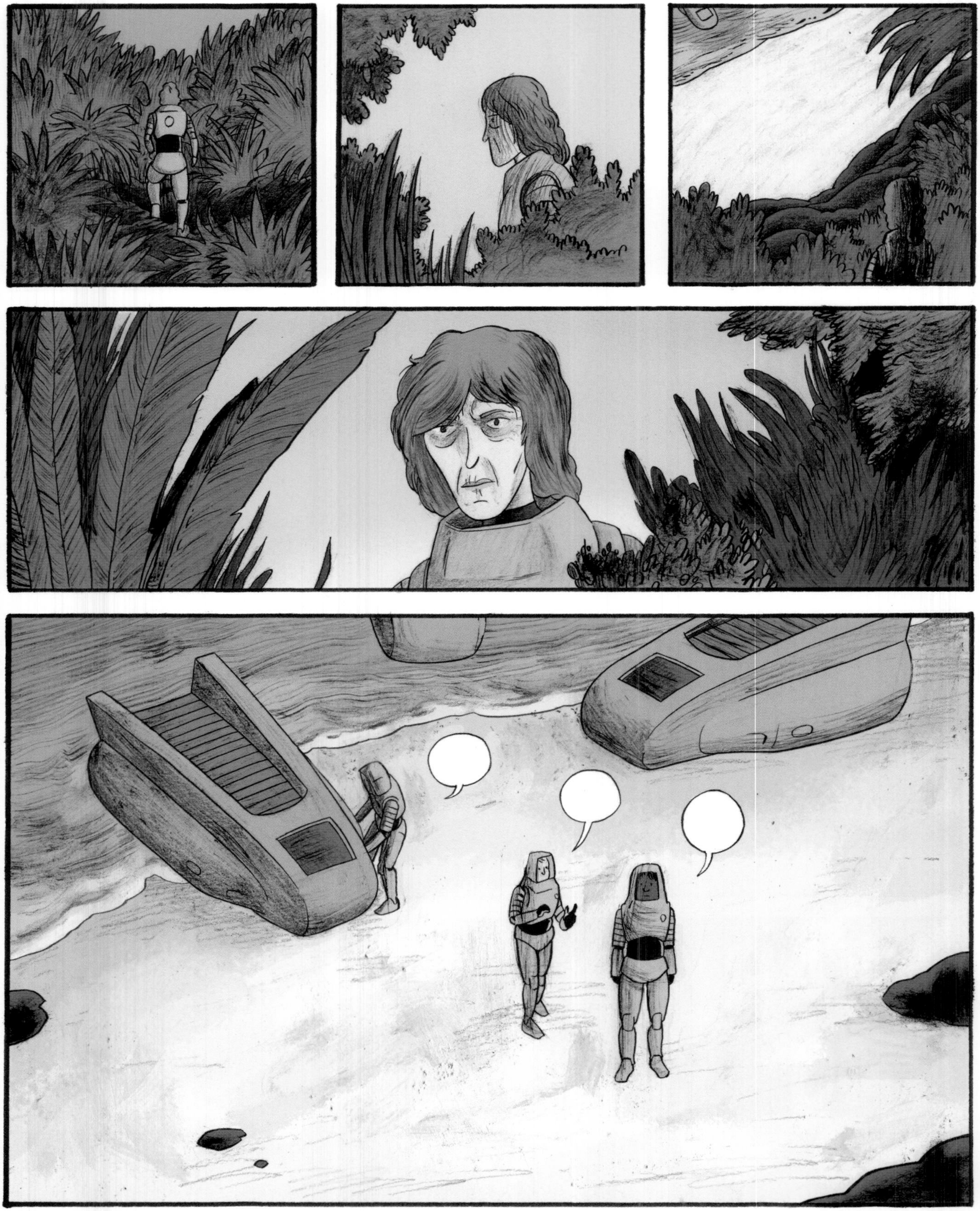

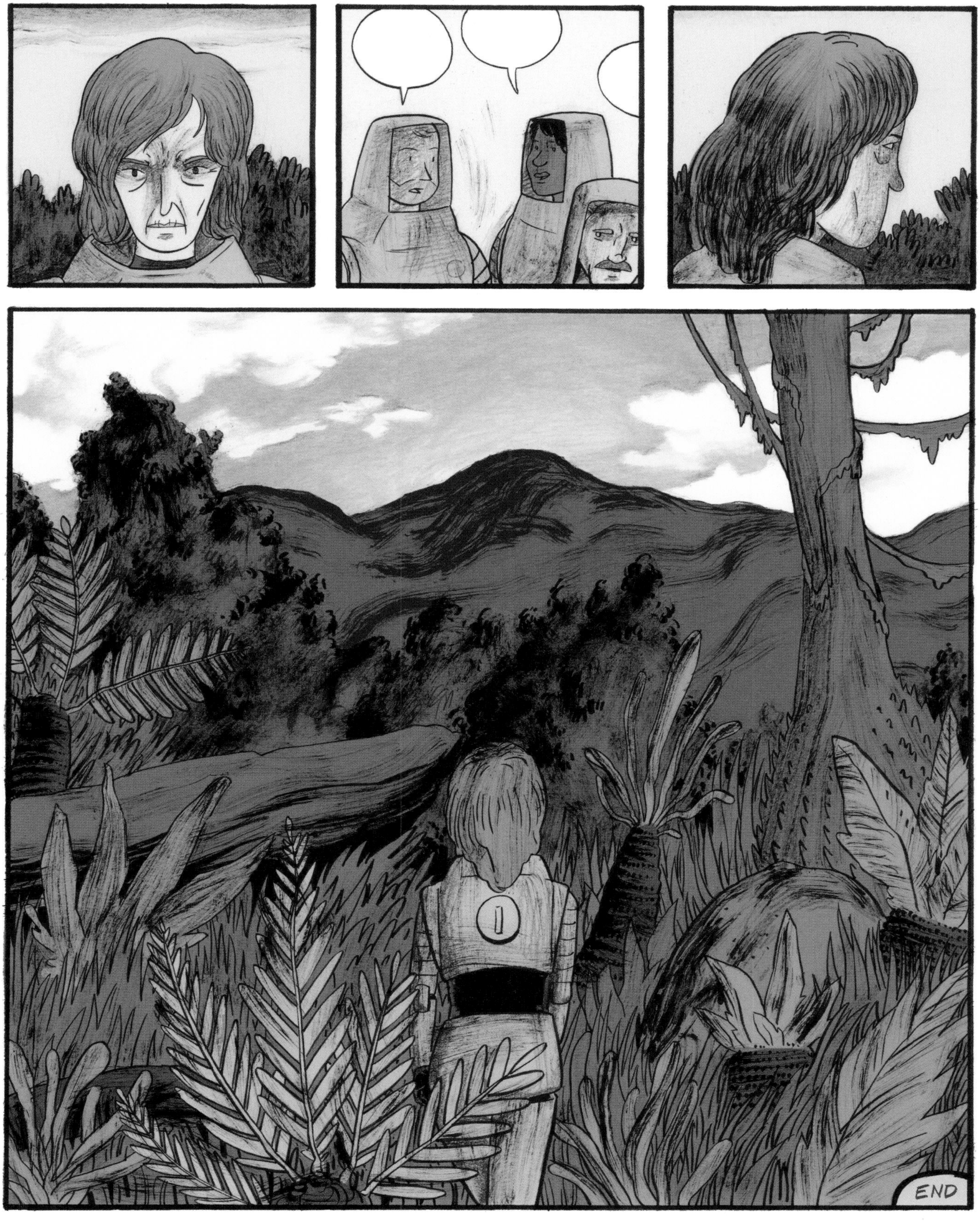
END

THE SCOUT

MALACHI WARD

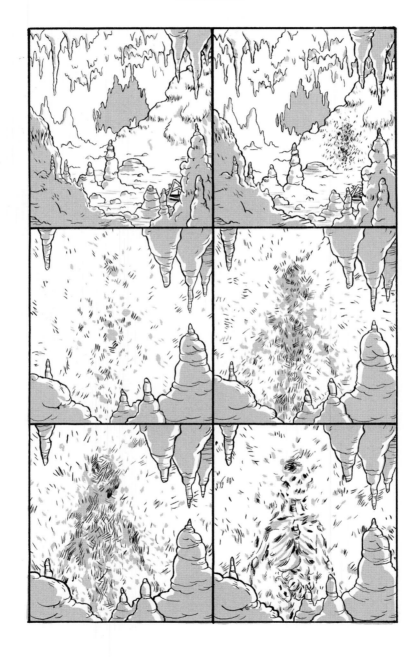

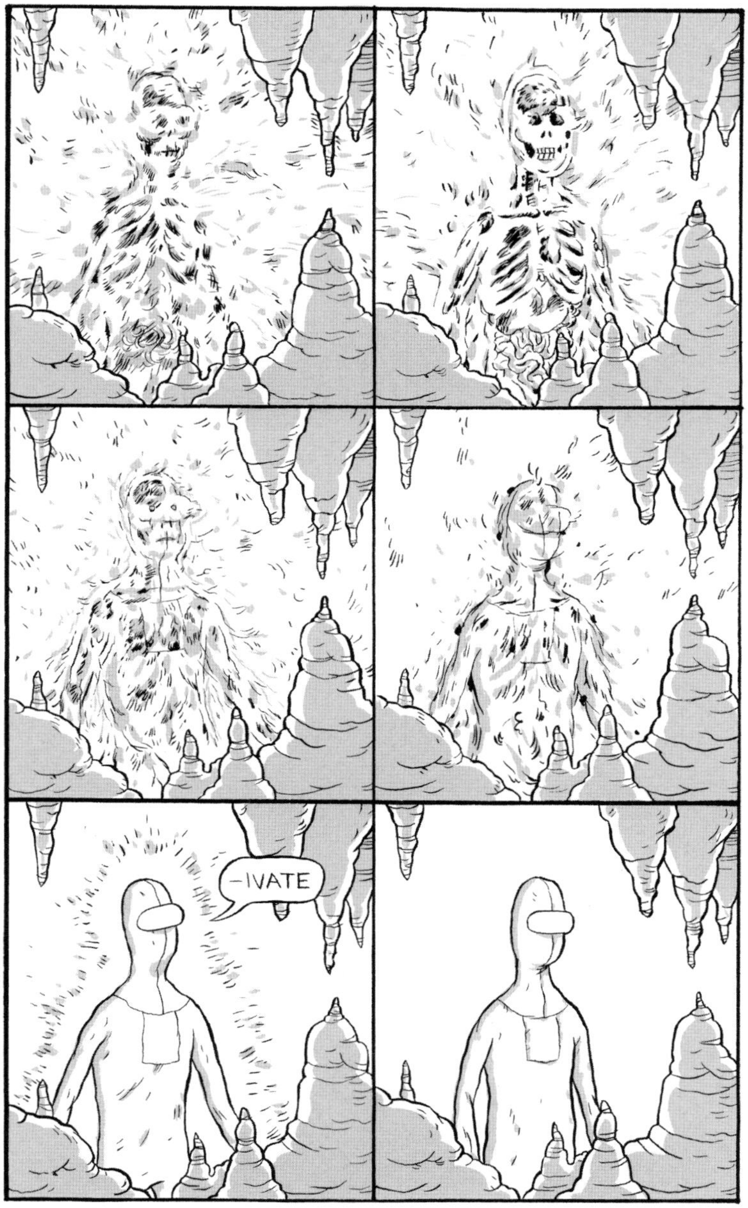
—IVATE

123

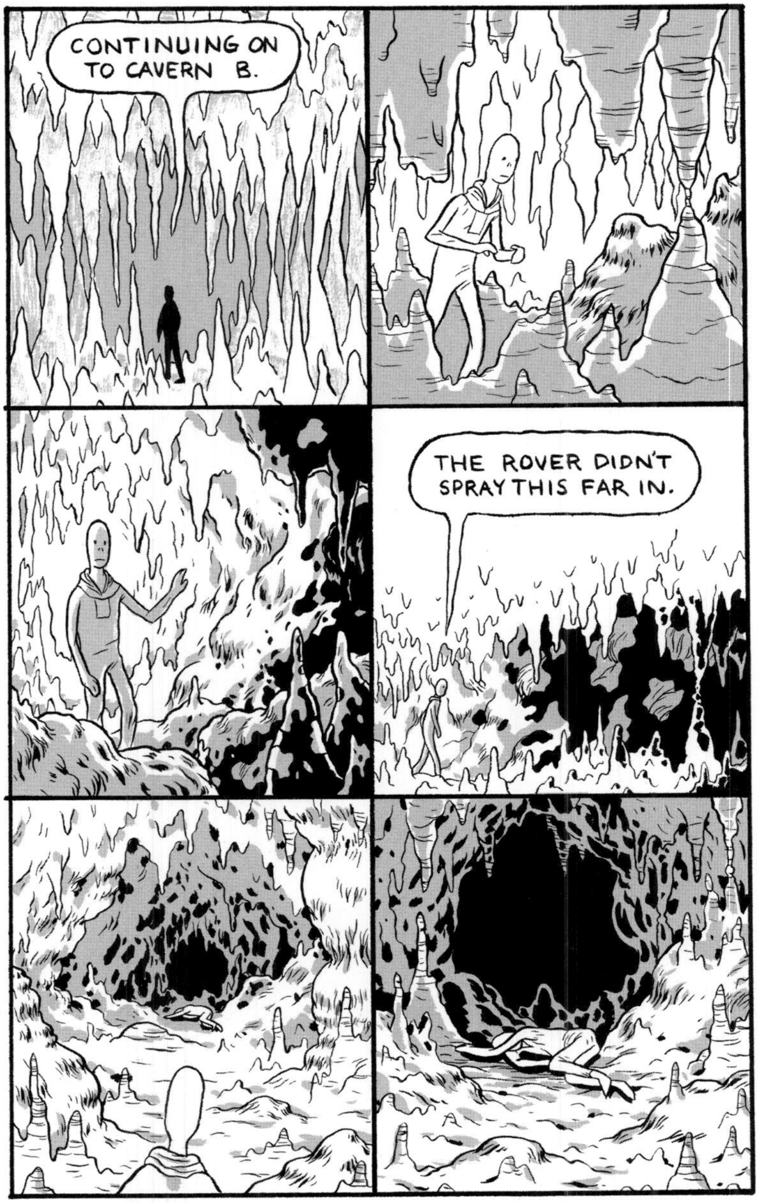
CONTINUING ON TO CAVERN B.
THE ROVER DIDN'T SPRAY THIS FAR IN.

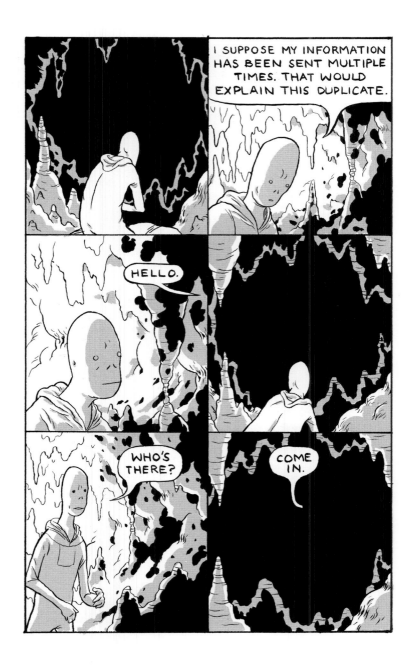

127

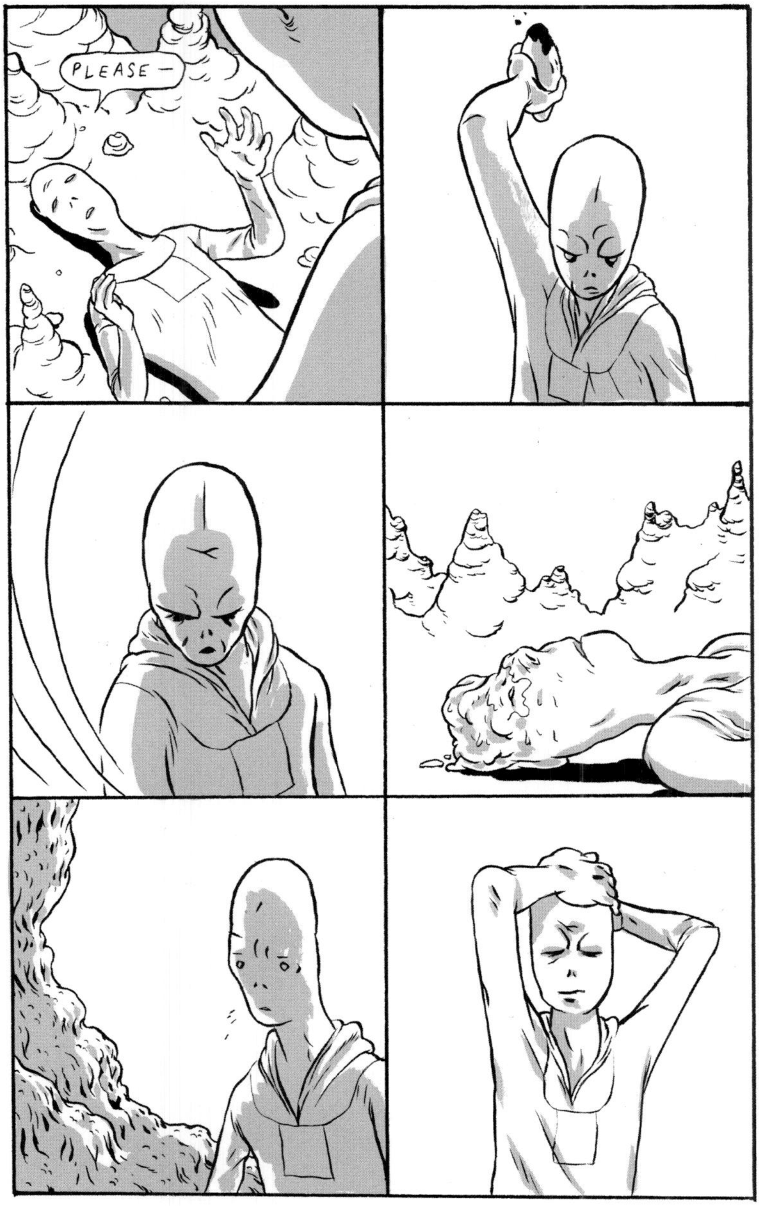
PLEASE —

-IVATE
THE END

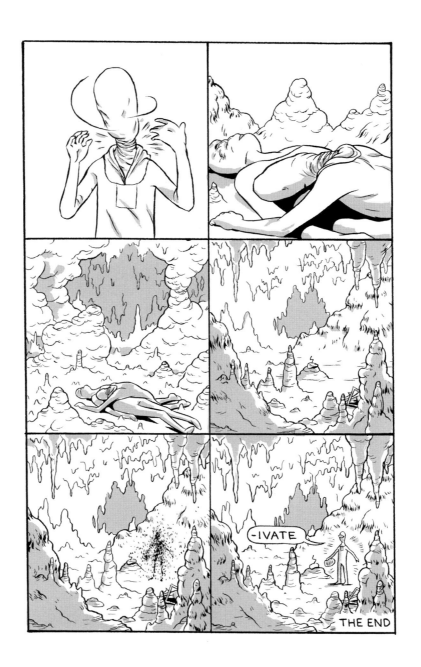

SWEET DREAMS

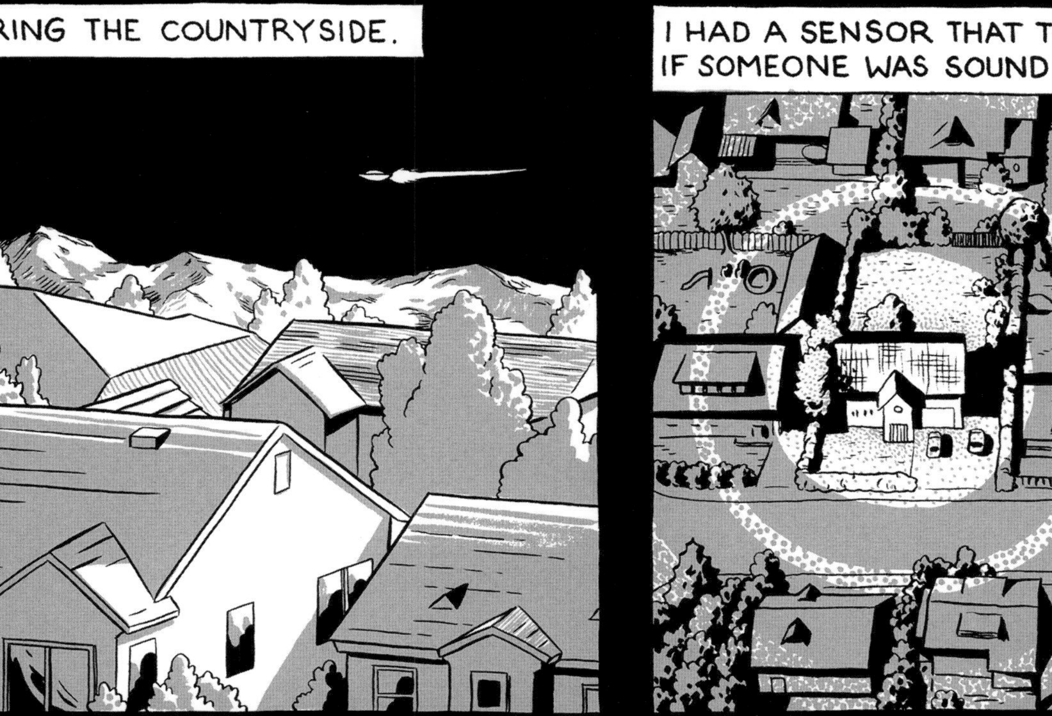
RING THE COUNTRYSIDE.
I HAD A SENSOR THAT T
IF SOMEONE WAS SOUND

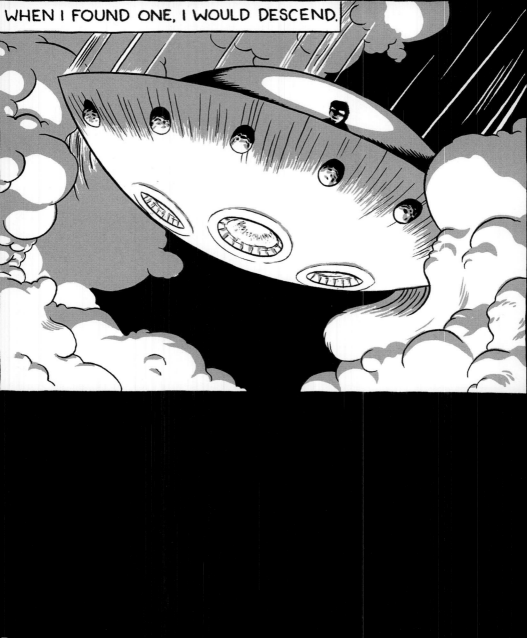

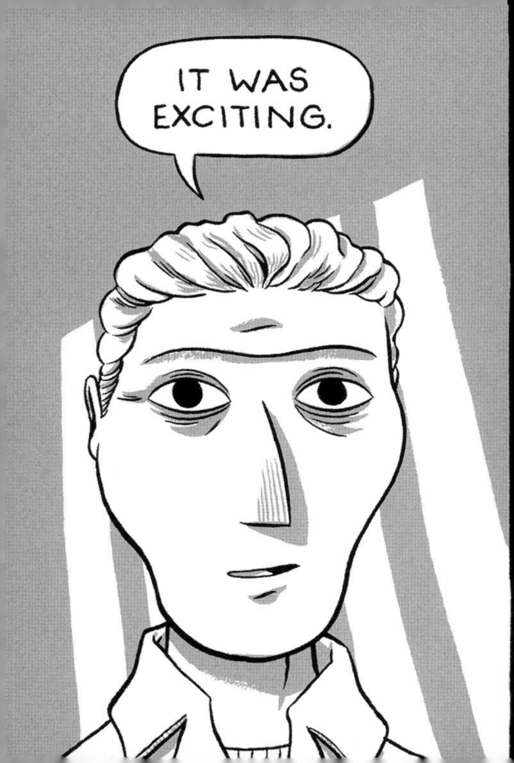
IT WAS EXCITING.

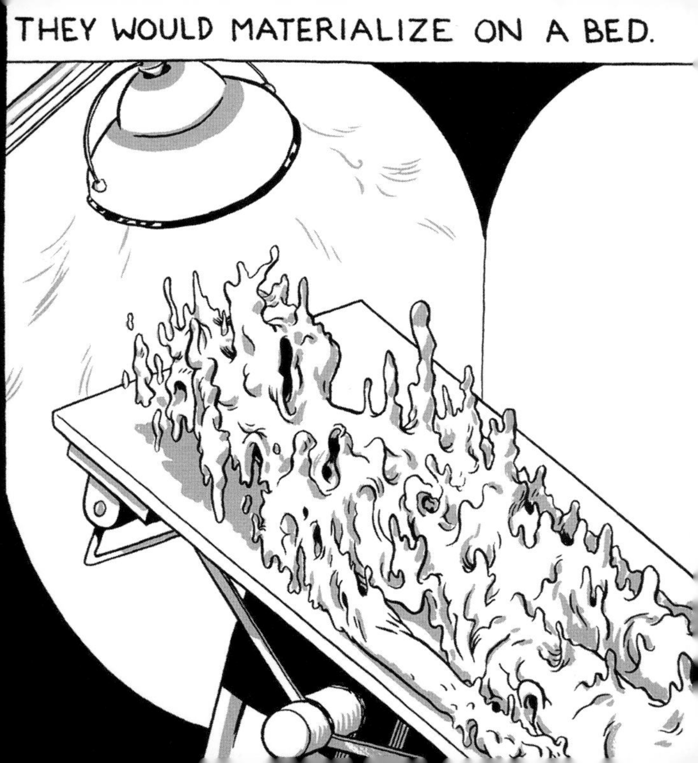
THEY WOULD MATERIALIZE ON A BED.

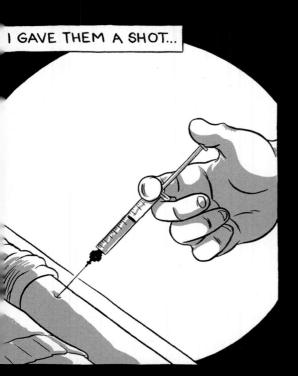

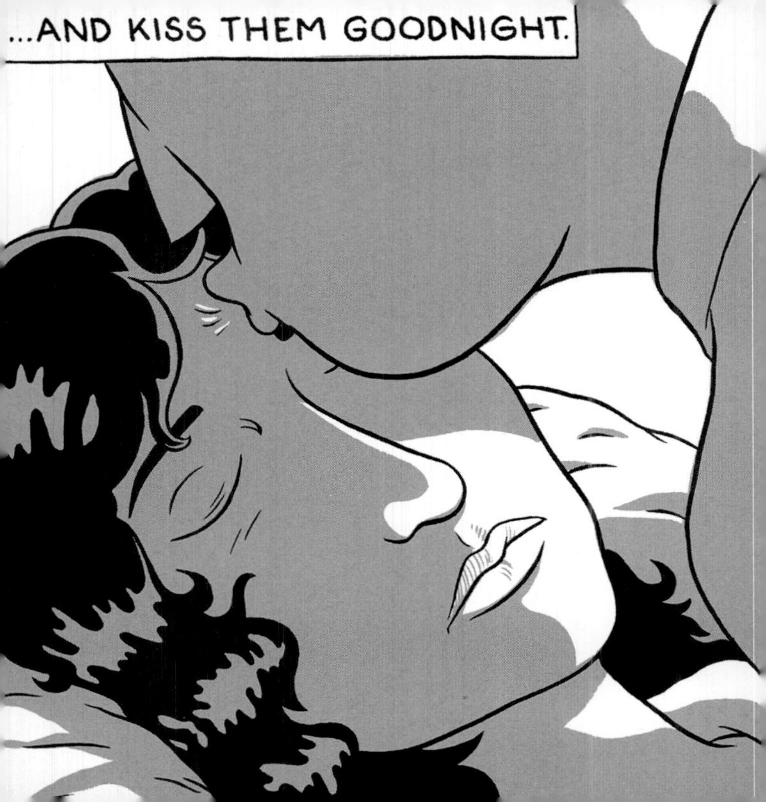
...AND KISS THEM GOODNIGHT.

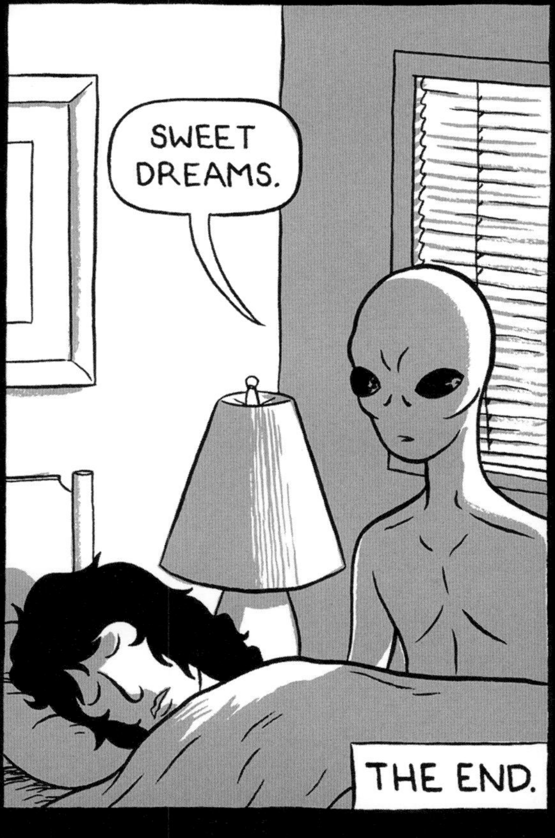
SWEET DREAMS.
THE END.

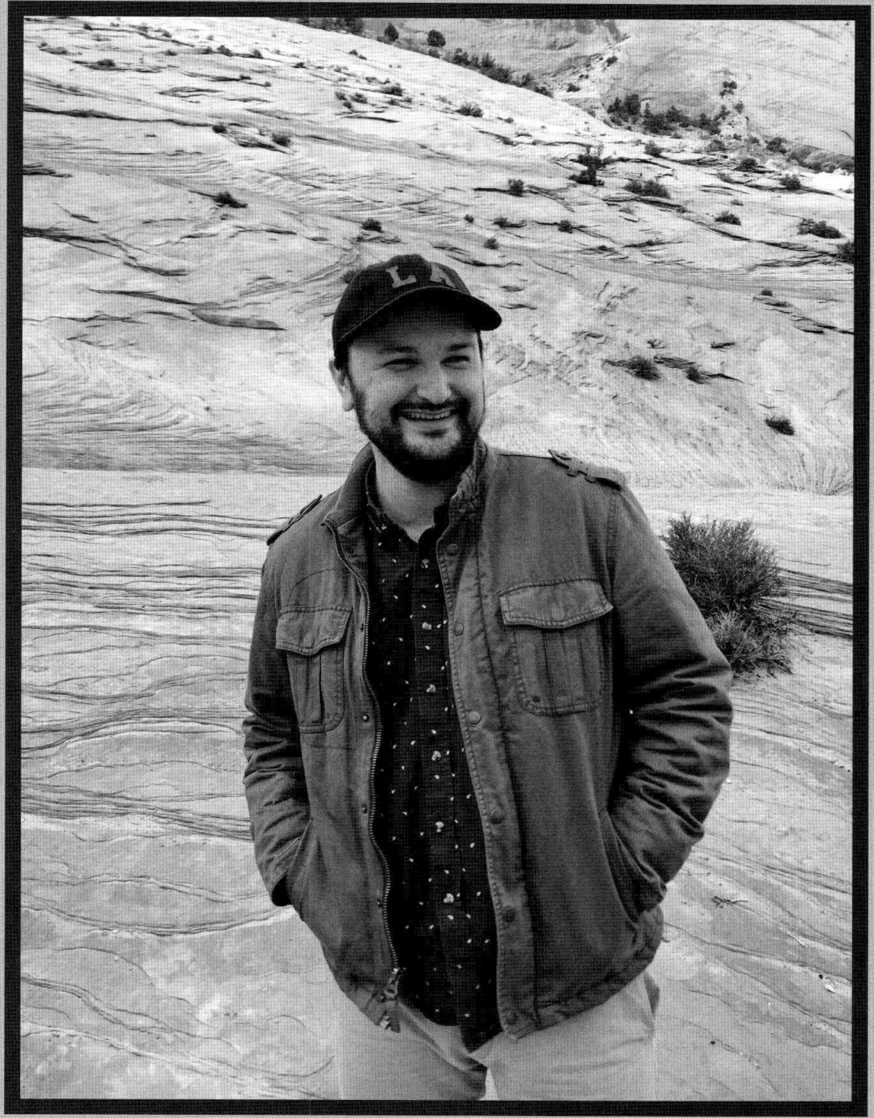
LA

Malachi Ward is the creator of the *Ritual* comic book series for Revival House Press, The *Expansion* series with Matt Sheean, *The Scout, Utu*, and *Top Five*, which is included in the 2013 edition of *Best American Comics*. Malachi has done work for Brandon Graham's *Prophet*, *Mome*, *NoBrow*, *Island*, and *Study Group Magazine*.